DEBT REDUCTION
AND DEVELOPMENT

DEBT REDUCTION AND DEVELOPMENT

THE CASE OF MEXICO

SUDARSHAN GOOPTU

PRAEGER

Westport, Connecticut
London

The findings, interpretations and conclusions in this work are the author's own. They should not, in any way, be attributed to the World Bank, members of its Board of Executive Directors, its management, or any of its member countries.

Copyright Acknowledgments

Permission granted by the respective publishers to include in this book extracts from the following publications is greatly appreciated:

International Monetary Fund, *World Economic Outlook 1990*, October 1990.

World Bank, *World Debt Tables, 1989-90*, December 1990.

Library of Congress Cataloging-in-Publication Data

Gooptu, Sudarshan.
    Debt reduction and development : the case of Mexico / Sudarshan Gooptu.
        p.   cm.
    Includes bibliographical references (p.   ) and index.
    ISBN 0-275-94213-9 (alk. paper)
    1. Debt relief—Mexico.   I. Title.
    HJ8519.G66   1993
    336.3'4'0972—dc20   92-3725

British Library Cataloguing in Publication Data is available.

Library of Congress Catalog Card Number: 92-3725
ISBN: 0-275-94213-9

First published in 1993

Praeger Publishers, 88 Post Road West, Westport, CT 06881
An imprint of Greenwood Publishing Group, Inc.

Printed in the United States of America

∞™

The paper used in this book complies with the Permanent Paper Standard issued by the National Information Standards Organization (Z39.48-1984).

10 9 8 7 6 5 4 3 2 1

To Mother, Father and Toneema

Contents

Tables

APPENDIXES

Charts

APPENDIXES

Acknowledgments

First and foremost, I would like to thank Professor Werner Baer, whose encouragement and expertise on developmental issues, in general, and Latin America, in particular, sparked my interest in learning more about these countries. His patience and understanding, as well as constructive guidance, made this endeavor a fruitful one. I am grateful to Mr. Jesus Silva Herzog for providing me access to key individuals at the Banco de Mexico, Hacienda, and SPP. The quality of this study was greatly enhanced by the deep and meaningful insights of the professors at the Colegio de Mexico and ITAM, especially the late Dr. Miguel Wionczek, as well as my numerous friends in Mexico. I sincerely appreciate the warmth and friendship extended by the Arreola-Cavazos family, who made me feel at home in Mexico. I would like to thank the Tinker Foundation and the Graduate College of the University of Illinois, Urbana-Champaign, for providing financial support for my initial research in Mexico. I thank Dr. Masood Ahmed and Dr. John Shilling for their encouraging me to take this endeavor through to its culmination. I thank my current colleagues at the International Economics Department and my former colleagues in the Cofinancing and Financial Advisory Services Department of the World Bank for giving me the opportunity to keep abreast of recent developments in the area of International Debt of the developing world and for my participating effectively in the developing country debt workout process. Their insights and cooperation are greatly appreciated.

I wish to thank Professors Hadi Esfahani and William Maloney for their comments and constructive suggestions on earlier versions of this manuscript. I would like to thank Maria Queen for her undivided attention and cooperation in typing the manuscript, and Hong Vo for the excellent job she did in getting the manuscript into camera-ready form. Their adherence to short deadlines was sincerely appreciated. The production of this book was also made possible due to the pertinent editorial comments and suggestions from the production editors at Praeger.

Finally, I am deeply indebted to Toneema, who gave me the strength to consistently work towards my immediate goal of completing my book and for putting up with me during my trials and tribulations. I am also indebted to my late mother and my father for encouraging me to strive for higher learning and for letting me go when it was time to do so. The moral support of my sister in this regard is also appreciated.

Introduction

A decade has gone by since the International Debt Crisis came to the forefront of academic debates and policy dilemmas facing less developed countries (LDCs), when Mexico declared a moratorium on debt service payments to its commercial bank creditors. Looking at the vast body of literature that has emerged on the subject during this period, one would have expected the problem to have been effectively tackled by now. However, this is not the reality of the situation. The debt problems of most developing countries continue to persist.

The number of countries facing debt-servicing difficulties on their external obligations has increased between 1982 and 1990 to such an extent that the World Bank, in its 1989-90 "World Debt Tables," has broken them up into separate groups (i.e., severely indebted middle-income countries [SIMICs], severely indebted low-income countries [SILICs], and moderately indebted middle-income and low-income country groups). The results of the stringent adjustment programs in the highly indebted countries (HICs) have been mixed with most countries, at best being at the same situation they were in prior to the crisis in terms of their macroeconomic indicators. On the creditors' side, there have been retrenchment and consolidation of their LDC portfolios, and changes in their host country's tax, regulatory, and accounting regimes. This has resulted in a greater diversity in the remaining commercial bank creditor preferences, so that any particular way of tackling the LDC debt problem (e.g., a debt write-off/buyback) that may be attractive for one group of commercial bank creditors, may not be so for another group of banks.

On the debtors' side, the previous initiatives for dealing with their debt problems that have been applied have left them with a large debt overhang, which has led to the emergence of negative incentive effects inducing private investors not to invest in their country for fear that their future returns from such investment would be taxed by the Government in some form or the other in order for it to make debt service payments to its external creditors.

The objective of this study is to address simultaneously both these issues facing the debtor country and its commercial bank creditors in order to move a step closer towards understanding the situation--putting the pieces of the puzzle of the International Debt Crisis together--so as to see the big picture. The premise this book proceeds from is the need to examine the situation on a *case-by-case* basis and, thereby, move a step closer to solving the debt crisis facing developing nations.

According to the World Bank's "World Debt Tables," 1991-92, the task of resolving the external debt problem of LDCs is far from over.[1] For the severely indebted low- and lower middle-income countries, the external debt burdens remain unsustainably high. The stock of external debt owed by developing countries, as a whole, was estimated to be $1,281 billion in 1991, unchanged from their level a year earlier. The growth of output in developing countries was weak in both 1990 and 1991, and *per capita* output growth even worse. Gross domestic product (GDP) grew at 1.8 percent in 1991 as opposed to 1.9 percent in 1990 and 3.2 percent in 1989. Growth in world trade has slowed in the past two years, and the terms of trade have become unfavorable for the developing countries. This has partly resulted in sluggish export growth that has had an adverse effect on the debt indicators of these LDCs.

In a recent report of the World Bank entitled *Global Economic Prospects and the Developing Countries, 1992*, the outlook for the 1990s appear to be mixed. Output is expected to grow at 2.6 percent per annum, on average, in the major industrialized nations. A rate of growth which is slower than that in the 1980s. Real interest rates in the 1990s are expected to remain high (at around 3 percent) and commodity prices are expected to remain at current low levels. With the increased demand for external finance, partly because of the financing needs of the Eastern European countries and those of the former Soviet Union (FSU) and increased budgetary restrictions in donor countries, external financing on concessional terms will become scarce. The recent experiences of Chile, Mexico and Venezuela show one to expect that private capital flows will primarily be directed to countries with strong credit worthiness and a track record of sustained growth-oriented policy reforms.

Evaluation of the International Debt Crisis begins with a brief overview of the trends in external indebtedness of the developing countries, in general, and those in Latin America, in particular. In Chapter 1, the general characteristics of the debt problem are presented in some detail, along with a survey of the proposals that have been recommended in the ongoing endeavor to solve the International Debt Crisis. In Chapter 2, the external debt situation of our case at hand--Mexico--is evaluated by providing appropriate data, along with a critical evaluation of the developments that led to the declaration of the moratorium in August 1982. A brief study of the pre-1973 period is also provided in order to exhibit fully the initial conditions that existed at the eve of the period under consideration in this study (1973-89).

The developments after Mexico's 1982 moratorium are examined in Chapter 3. Three aspects are highlighted in the discussion:

1. The domestic policies and adjustment efforts on the part of the Mexican government to rejuvenate public confidence and incentives to bring about the return of capital flight, increased investment, and growth.

2. The role and trends of direct foreign investment in Mexico.

3. The developments in Mexico's debt renegotiation process, including the most recent (1988-89) commercial bank debt and debt service reduction (DDSR) package that Mexico finalized in order to deal with its debt problem in a comprehensive manner, keeping the diverse interests of its commercial bank creditors in mind. Mexico was the first country to benefit from the official support provided under the auspices of the *Brady Initiative*.

A brief survey of the theoretical literature on the International Debt Crisis is provided in Chapter 4, along with an intertemporal welfare maximizing model in which the *debt overhang* argument put forward in the recent debates on the debt crisis is examined. Within this framework, conditions (in the form of reduced form equations) are derived to compare a debt buyback (with alternative sources of financing) with a concessional rescheduling of existing debt obligations in the context of a DDSR package consisting of a market-based menu of options.

Empirical findings on the basis of both a casual empiricism (using charts) and a multivariate regression analysis are provided after an examination of the hypothesis that Mexico does lie on the wrong side of the "Debt-Laffer Curve," implying that the level of external debt is causing a negative "incentive effect" on gross domestic capital formation in the Mexican private sector. General conclusions of this study of the Mexican case are provided thereafter.

NOTE

1. See World Bank, "World Debt Tables," 1991-92, pp.3-12.

1

The International Debt Crisis:
An Overview

The International Debt Crisis has been one of the most important issues that has concerned academics and policy makers who are associated with the LDCs for a decade. This is quite apparent from the staggering amount of literature that has been published in this area of study. The problem still persists, although both debtor countries and creditor groups have been trying in earnest to work their way out of this problem through lengthy discussions and the implementation of innovative proposals. As recently as September 1990, the Government of Great Britain proposed the "Trinidad Terms" to deal with the debt of the severely indebted low-income countries that is owed to official bilateral creditors. It was proposed that the Paris Club creditors forgive a part of the total stock of debt owed by the low-income debt-distressed nations rather than merely the debt service payments falling due during the consolidation period (along with outstanding arrears), as is the current practice on the basis of the "Toronto Terms." In the arena of commercial bank debt, the current prescription (under the auspices of the "Brady Initiative") is to embark on DDSR by formulating "packages" that contain a market-based menu of options. Some of these instruments are supported by official agencies, such as the World Bank and the IMF, so as to be catalysts in the comprehensive settlement of a country's debt problem --at least for now and the medium term.

This chapter provides an overview of the trends in external indebtedness of the developing countries, in general, and those in Latin America, in particular. The general characteristics of the Debt Problem are presented in some detail along with a survey of the proposals that have been recommended in the ongoing endeavor to solve the International Debt

Crisis. What will become clear from this discussion is the need to proceed with an evaluation of the problem on a *case-by-case* basis. Global solutions to the problem are not the answer. A critical examination of the major actors (both debtor countries and creditor groups) is necessary in order to identify and put together the necessary pieces of the puzzle to see the big picture. On a global basis, however, three common themes seem to appear over and over again in the debates:

1. A debt overhang exists in the severely indebted countries which is an impediment to increasing investment and growth in these countries.

2. Both debtor countries and creditor groups were involved in bringing about the debt crisis, and both parties must work together to find a way out of it. This includes the involvement of the host governments of the creditor banks in providing an appropriate regulatory framework to curtail the massive flow of funds into only a few countries (e.g., Mexico, after the oil boom) and, at the same time, provide adequate mechanisms in order to enable banks to grant debt relief to these HICs.

3. For the severly indebted low-and lower-middle-income countries there is the need for greater official support on highly concessional terms as well as significant debt forgiveness of existing obligations beyond those suggested by the "Trinidad terms".

We begin our discussion by observing the trends in international lending to the Third World nations to date. In the next section, the question that faces most of the severely indebted countries (low income or middle income), at some time or the other, is examined--whether they should default on their debt service obligations to external creditors or not. A brief survey of the proposals that have been suggested in the profession to deal with the debt crisis is provided in the following section. The critical impediment of the debt overhang that has emerged in view of past developments is elaborated on in the subsequent section. A summary and conclusions are provided in the section thereafter.

TRENDS IN INTERNATIONAL LENDING TO LDCS

External borrowing allows a country to relax its constraints on domestic savings and foreign exchange in order to increase its rate of economic growth and to bring about economic development much faster than would otherwise be possible. Income-generating increases in capital stock are made possible if external borrowing takes place when the cost of capital in the international financial market is less than the marginal productivity of domestic capital. The availability of external borrowing opportunities initially allows imports to exceed exports and investment to exceed domestic savings. Repayment of these loans (principal and interest) will only be possible if these inequalities are reversed within a reasonable period of time determined by the conditions of the loans. The emergence of a debt problem can be avoided only if the borrower is successful in closing the domestic savings gap and, in turn, generating excess savings. Also, since the outstanding loans have to be repaid in foreign exchange, the borrower has to attempt to convert the excess savings into foreign exchange. This can be achieved by adopting policies that will eventually increase its exports relative to its imports. As the country develops, savings rates, the rate of capital accumulation, per capita income and rates of return on investment change so as to alter the rate and direction of international capital flows eventually.

Table 1.1 clearly shows the rapid increase in external borrowing by LDCs. This has led to an increase in the financial dependence of these debtor nations and brought with it associated debt-servicing difficulties. The magnitude of external debt of the LDCs has grown to such an extent that a debt overhang has emerged in the severely indebted countries, which tends to discourage private domestic investment and brings about uncertainties concerning the course of future monetary, fiscal, and exchange rate policies in these countries. This, in turn, induces capital flight and inhibits growth. Table 1.1 shows the rates of growth of external indebtedness by country groups between 1970-86. The period 1973-80 has experienced rapid growth in lending to developing countries. This trend has been observed for lending from official sources (i.e., loans from international organizations and from governments) as well as from private sources (i.e., export credit, credits from manufacturers and other suppliers of goods, loans from commercial banks and nonbank financial intermediaries, as well as publicly issued and privately placed bonds and other financial instruments). The rapid growth in external indebtedness of the developing countries during this period (1973-80) was especially concentrated in the middle-income countries (with 1987 GNP per capita of at least $480 per

Table 1.1

Growth of Long-Term External Debt of Developing Countries, 1970-80, 82-86
(average annual percentage change, nominal)

Country Group	1970-73	1973-80	1982	1983	1984	1985	1986
ALL DEVELOPING COUNTRIES	18.0	21.6	12.3	14.6	6.6	8.1	5.2
Official Creditors	15.4	17.4	10.6	12.0	7.0	13.7	5.5
Private Creditors	20.6	24.6	13.2	16.0	6.4	5.2	5.0
LOW-INCOME COUNTRIES	12.4	14.9	10.5	9.5	5.6	16.6	8.8
Official Creditors	12.4	14.5	10.4	10.9	4.7	16.3	8.7
Private Creditors	12.2	17.0	10.7	3.4	9.6	18.0	9.0
MIDDLE-INCOME COUNTRIES	19.6	22.9	12.6	15.3	6.8	6.9	4.6
Official Creditors	17.2	18.9	10.7	12.5	7.9	12.6	4.2
Private Creditors	21.2	25.0	13.3	16.5	6.3	4.7	4.8
HIGHLY-INDEBTED COUNTRIES	17.5	22.3	13.1	19.1	7.5	3.8	4.7
Official Creditors	13.3	14.8	11.8	19.4	11.0	14.4	4.8
Private Creditors	19.3	24.5	13.4	19.0	6.8	1.6	4.7

Source: World Bank, World Development Report, 1987, p. 176.

annum and less than $6,000 p.a.) where total debt outstanding and disbursed (in nominal terms) increased at an average rate of 22.9 percent per annum. The average annual rates of growth of long-term debt accumulation for this period from official sources and private sources were 18.9 percent and 25 percent, respectively. All the seventeen HICs, as classified by the World Bank,[1] are middle-income countries. Even though there has been a decline in lending to developing countries in general and middle-income countries after 1982, the rates of growth in external indebtedness continue to be high for the HICs.

The evidence presented in Table 1.2 shows a drastic shift in external lending to developing countries from commercial banks to official sources, especially between 1987-90. In the HICs, total debt owed to official creditors increased from a total of $131.5 billion in 1987 to $161.6 billion by 1990, whereas that owed by commercial banks fell from $298.8 billion in 1987 to $263.7 by 1990. This can be attributed to the increased involvement of the official agencies and governments in supporting DDSR packages, by providing credit enhancement (funds for principal collateralization and interest guarantees on exit bonds), and bridge loans from governments.

The year 1982 is a watershed in the international debt situation of developing countries. As shown in Table 1.3, after 1982 there has been a drastic reduction in net transfers going to developing countries.[2] In fact, the net transfers became negative from 1983 onwards for the HICs. This net outflow of resources from the HICs widens the foreign exchange gap, which, in turn, hampers economic growth and development in these countries. The future repayment capacity of the HICs and maintenance of their credit worthiness in the international financial markets are contingent on the success of the ongoing endeavor of these countries to bring about economic growth and attain higher standards of living for their people.

The magnitude of the total debt outstanding does not provide any information about the debt repayment capacity of the countries concerned. The burden of external debt of a country should be viewed in conjunction with its ability to repay its external creditors and the structure of the debt outstanding, specifically, maturity of the debt and the rate of interest charged. Therefore, other debt indicators are also used to illustrate the gravity of the external debt situation of a country.[3] Table 1.4 shows the debt service ratio (i.e., debt service to exports ratio) and ratio of interest payments to export earnings for developing countries between 1975 and 1989. For all the developing countries taken together, the debt service ratio has risen from 8.5 percent in 1975 to 27.5 percent in 1989. This ratio has been even higher for the SIMICs. It rose from 12.3 percent in 1975 to

Table 1.2
External Debt of the "Baker 15" Nations, 1982-90 (in billions of dollars)

Country Group	1982	1983	1984	1985	1986	1987	1988	1989	1990
By Maturity:									
ALL DEVELOPING COUNTRIES	839.2	889.3	931.8	1,004.6	1,098.6	1,220.3	1,234.8	1,237.0	1,302.6
Short-term	187.0	176.6	172.2	169.9	175.2	201.2	213.2	213.2	209.0
Medium & Long term	652.2	712.7	759.6	834.7	923.4	1,019.1	1,021.6	1,023.8	1,093.6
HIGHLY INDEBTED COUNTRIES1/	380.3	396.0	408.9	420.2	446.0	487.5	479.0	478.5	487.0
Short-term	75.3	57.3	47.2	39.6	36.8	41.9	43.1	43.0	36.9
Medium & Long term	305.0	338.7	361.7	380.6	409.2	445.6	435.9	435.5	450.1
By Creditor:									
ALL DEVELOPING COUNTRIES									
Official	249.4	280.3	304.3	354.1	410.5	489.0	500.4	514.1	560.6
Banks	433.7	463.6	476.8	495.5	521.4	559.8	541.7	527.3	533.5
Other Private	156.1	145.4	150.7	155.1	166.8	171.5	192.7	195.6	208.5
HIGHLY INDEBTED COUNTRIES1/									
Official	50.5	64.3	73.2	88.6	105.2	131.5	137.9	144.9	161.6
Banks	256.4	271.3	281.6	280.0	285.5	298.8	280.6	271.6	263.7
Other Private	73.4	60.4	54.1	51.6	55.3	57.3	60.6	62.0	61.7

Source: International Monetary Fund, World Economic Outlook, October 1990.

Note: 1. Includes the Baker 15 countries: Argentina, Bolivia, Brazil, Chile, Colombia, Cote d'Ivoire, Ecuador, Mexico, Morocco, Nigeria, Peru, Philippines, Uruguay, Venezuela and Yugoslavia.

Table 1.3
Trends in Debt-Related Flows, 1980-89 (US$ billions)

Country Group	1980	1981	1982	1983	1984	1985	1986	1987	1988	1989
NET FLOWS OF TOTAL EXTERNAL DEBT										
All developing countries1/	66.5	84.0	74.5	62.3	47.5	33.5	26.6	23.9	20.3	25.6
o/w. Severely Indebted	35.0	50.4	41.6	29.2	21.8	7.5	9.0	13.9	8.7	11.0
Low income	5.9	7.0	6.8	5.7	3.4	0.7	3.6	3.9	2.4	3.8
Middle income	29.1	43.4	34.8	23.5	18.4	6.8	5.4	10.0	6.3	7.2
Moderately Indebted	15.4	14.9	14.7	15.2	11.7	13.1	12.5	10.1	6.2	10.4
Low income	3.9	4.7	6.0	6.2	4.2	3.3	4.3	5.5	4.4	4.5
Middle income	11.5	10.2	8.7	9.0	7.5	9.8	8.2	4.6	1.8	5.9
NET TRANSFERS OF TOTAL EXTERNAL DEBT										
All developing countries 1/	19.6	22.7	6.4	(2.4)	(21.9)	(36.2)	(38.2)	(40.3)	(52.0)	(51.6)
o/w. Severely indebted	5.4	11.2	(2.0)	(11.1)	(19.9)	(33.8)	(26.4)	(19.7)	(31.3)	(31.6)
Low income	3.7	4.4	4.3	3.0	0.2	(2.4)	1.3	1.9	(0.5)	1.0
Middle income	1.7	6.8	(6.3)	(14.1)	(20.1)	(31.4)	(27.7)	(21.6)	(30.8)	(32.6)
Moderately indebted	6.3	3.2	2.0	2.6	(2.7)	(0.9)	(2.7)	(5.6)	(10.9)	(8.0)
Low income	1.9	2.4	3.3	3.4	0.8	(0.1)	0.4	1.0	(0.3)	(0.7)
Middle income	4.4	0.8	(1.3)	(0.8)	(3.5)	(0.8)	(3.1)	(6.6)	(10.6)	(7.3)

Source: World Bank, "World Debt Tables", 1989-90, p. 9 (Table 2).
1. DRS reporting countries
( ) Negative net flows from abroad

Table 1.4
Debt Service Ratios for Total Debt of Developing Countries, 1975-89 (percent)

Country Group and Item	1975	1980	1982	1983	1984	1985	1986	1987	1988	1989
DEVELOPING COUNTRIES*										
Debt Service Ratio (%)	8.5	21.4	27.3	26.3	26.1	30.4	32.5	29.0	28.5	27.5
Ratio of Interest Payments to Export Earnings	3.2	10.8	15.8	15.4	15.2	15.5	14.9	12.6	12.9	13.0
MIDDLE-INCOME COUNTRIES										
Debt Service Ratio (%)	8.7	25.5	31.0	29.0	28.4	32.8	34.7	30.9	29.7	28.6
Ratio of Interest Payments to Export Earnings	3.3	13.0	18.3	17.5	17.0	17.4	16.3	13.5	13.5	13.7
LOW-INCOME COUNTRIES										
Debt Service Ratio (%)	7.6	9.8	14.6	17.2	18.2	22.4	24.8	22.1	24.3	23.8
Ratio of Interest Payments to Export Earnings	2.8	4.7	7.3	8.1	8.9	9.3	10.0	9.7	10.6	10.7
SEVERELY INDEBTED MIDDLE INCOME*										
Debt Service Ratio (%)	12.3	37.1	46.8	40.5	38.0	42.3	44.6	38.2	38.2	40.9
Ratio of Interest Payments to Export Earnings	4.9	19.2	29.6	27.4	25.7	26.45	25.3	21.8	22.3	24.4

Source: World Bank, "World Debt Tables," various issues: Washington, D.C.
Note: Total debt includes long-term, short-term, and use of IMF credits.
* Defined by the World Bank (19 countries).

Chart 1.1
External Debt of LDCs by Creditor Group, 1982-90

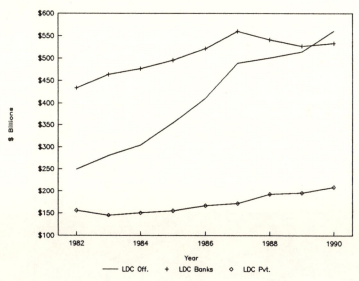

Chart 1.2
External Debt of Baker 15 by Creditor Group, 1982-90

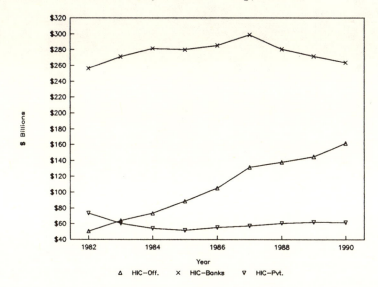

Chart 1.3
External Debt Flows to LDCs, 1980-89

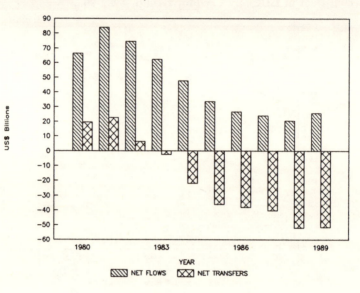

Chart 1.4
External Debt Flows, 1980-89: Severely Indebted Middle-Income Nations

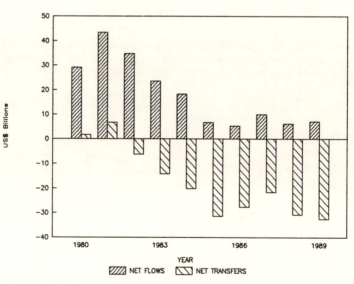

about 41 percent in 1989. The ratio of interest payments to export earnings rose from 3.2 percent in 1975 to 13 percent in 1989 for developing countries taken as a whole. For SIMICs, this ratio rose from 4.9 percent in 1975 to 24.4 percent by 1989.

The behavior of the debt service ratio provides an indication of the rigidity in a country's balance of payments and its dependence on export earnings to service its debt. However, the debt service ratio does not provide any information about the *ability* of the country to service its debt, the structure of the debt, the composition and geographical concentration of its exports, and the possibilities for expansion of the market for its exportables. Neither does the debt service ratio allow us to make inferences about the variability of export earnings, the level of foreign exchange reserves, and the scope for import-substitution as a way of increasing the net foreign exchange earnings corresponding to a given level of exports. In this way, the debt service ratio may exaggerate the magnitude of the debt problem by highlighting the exogenous constraints faced by the debtor countries.

Given the possibility of postponing repayment of the principal by multiple rescheduling of the debt, the immediate problem faced by the debtor country is payment of the interest on its outstanding debt. The ratio of interest payments to export earnings would then be an appropriate indicator of the liquidity aspect of the external debt situation of a country. Between 1975 and 1989, this ratio has more than quadrupled for the SIMICs (4.9 percent to 24.4 percent). It is also important to observe the behavior of net transfers in order to evaluate the future repayment capacity of the country concerned. The existence of a negative net transfer (as observed in Table 1.3) implies a pattern of capital flow that tends to widen the foreign exchange gap. This makes it difficult for the debtor to divert more resources to bring about economic growth and development in the long run, and maintain its credit worthiness in the international financial system.

As the situation stands today, there exist a large number of developing countries which have borrowed so much from abroad that their current economic situation prevents them from paying the interest on their debt obligations, let alone the principal. Table 1.5 shows the total debt outstanding and disbursed (DOD) at year-end 1989 for the nineteen SIMICs (as defined by the World Bank). The burden of external debt is quite unequal across the developing countries. First, there are the few large debtors (i.e., Brazil, Mexico, Argentina, Poland, Venezuela, Philippines) that are causing continuous concern to the international financial community, especially the large money center banks. Then, there are the countries

Table 1.5
The Severely Indebted Middle-Income Countries

Country	Debt Outstanding (end 1989)		AVERAGE ANNUAL GROWTH RATES, 1982-88 (percent)				
	TOTAL (US$ Bn.)	From Private Sources (%)	GDP	Exports	Imports	Invest- ment	Consump- tion Per capita
Argentina	61.9	74.3	0.9	2.3	0.6	(2.7)	(0.1)
Bolivia	5.8	12.2	(1.0)	1.5	4.6	(5.0)	(2.7)
Brazil	112.7	75.2	4.7	5.6	(1.4)	2.6	2.4
Chile	18.5	68.8	4.6	7.0	4.6	15.4	0.4
Congo	4.2	53.4	(0.7)	3.3	(10.2)	(15.2)	(2.8)
Costa Rica	4.6	47.4	3.8	1.9	9.3	9.1	3.5
Côte d'Ivoire	14.0	61.6	0.5	(3.0)	(7.0)	(7.6)	(3.4)
Ecuador	11.5	51.1	2.2	6.6	(1.0)	(20.0)	(1.5)
Honduras	3.4	22.3	2.8	2.9	4.6	7.7	(1.0)
Hungary	17.9	87.4	1.4	3.9	3.0	0.4	1.4
Mexico	102.9	76.0	0.2	4.7	1.6	(5.0)	(1.5)
Morocco	20.8	26.2	4.1	6.1	1.1	0.1	0.9

	Debt Outstanding (end 1989)		AVERAGE ANNUAL GROWTH RATES, 1982-88 (percent)				
Country	TOTAL (US$ Bn.)	From Private Sources (%)	GDP	Exports	Imports	Investment	Consumption Per capita
Nicaragua	8.6	19.6	(0.7)	(12.9)	0.8	2.0	(1.5)
Peru	19.9	43.0	2.1	(1.8)	(4.5)	(2.4)	0.6
Philippines	28.5	56.1	(0.2)	6.3	2.5	(10.7)	(0.2)
Poland	40.1	31.2	4.5	5.5	6.3	3.5	3.8
Senegal	3.6	15.5	2.5	(1.3)	(3.5)	1.7	(1.5)
Uruguay	4.5	79.1	1.8	4.6	1.5	(4.0)	1.3
Venezuela	34.1	94.7	2.1	6.0	1.2	2.1	(2.1)
TOTAL	517.5	65.4	2.5	4.8	1.3	(0.7)	0.4

Source: World Bank, "World Debt Tables", 1989-90, p. 30 (Box Table 7).

NOTE: The World Bank defines "severely indebted" countries as those with debt to GDP ratio greater than 50 percent, debt to exports ratio of 275 percent, accrued debt service to exports greater than 30 percent and accrued interest to exports to 20 percent.

with external indebtedness that is large in proportion to their domestic capacity to repay, but not large enough to precipitate a crisis in the international financial system (e.g., Bolivia, Peru, Ecuador, Chile, Costa Rica, Côte d'Ivoire, Honduras, Hungary, Nicaragua, Senegal and Zaire). Only a few of these countries possess the economic infrastructure to bring about economic growth, expansion of exports, and repayment of their external debt. Finally, there are those countries that include the poorest nations in the world (e.g., Benin, Comoro, Ghana, Liberia, and Niger among others) and that are not large debtors in terms of their debt outstanding but are regarded as poor credit risks by commercial banks. However, these countries are influenced by developments in the international financial system. Most of the debt outstanding to this group of countries is at concessional rates, and is owed to governments and other official creditors.

The geographical concentration of international indebtedness of LDCs is quite apparent from the fact that twelve of the nineteen severely indebted middle-income countries (World Bank definition) are in Latin America. Four countries (Argentina, Brazil, Mexico, and Venezuela) accounted for $311.3 billion out of $517.5 billion of total debt outstanding in the SIMICs in 1989 (Table 1.5). Most of the debt outstanding in SIMICs has been obtained from private sources. Not only has the debt outstanding in the SIMICs been borrowed from private sources but the *number* of private creditors who have significant exposure to Third World countries are few. For example, in the United States, the nine largest money center banks had loaned out 275 percent of their capital to developing countries in 1981 (Table 1.6).

After 1982, banks have reduced their exposure to developing countries, but the degree of exposure still continues to be high, especially for the nine largest money center banks. According to Rudiger Dornbusch--"A complete Latin write-off of debts would wipe out the large banks but would keep smaller ones intact. This is one of the senses in which the LDC debts are a 'Big Bank' problem" [Dornbusch (1986), p. 7]. William Cline supports this contention by stating that "large losses on LDC debt could cause technical insolvency of these banks" [Cline (1985), p. 185]. Others have taken the extreme view that "the default of one of these countries could shake the entire financial system; their collective default could bring it down" [Debt Crisis Network (1985), p. 7].[4]

The situation in the international financial system in the 1980s is being compared to the crisis of the 1930s. The rapid growth in external indebtedness of nations and the central role of a major economic power of the era are emphasized. In this context Rosemary Thorp and Laurence

Table 1.6
U.S. Bank Exposure to Developing Countries (as a percentage of capital)

Lending from:	1980	1981	1982	1983	1984	1985	1986
ALL COMMERCIAL BANKS							
All LDCs	159.7	183.3	177.1	159.5	134.4	108.6	91.3
Latin America	109.4	125.2	118.8	106.0	93.5	77.3	68.0
NINE LARGEST MONEY CENTER BANKS							
All LDCs	246.0	275.8	271.2	249.2	212.7	173.2	146.9
Latin America	163.3	179.9	176.5	162.9	146.4	124.2	110.2

Source: Federal Financial Institutions Examination Council, "Statistical Release" various issues.

Whitehead have stated:

> The heady lending of the 1920s represented the inexperience of the
> newly dominant creditor country, the U.S.A., the lending of the
> 1970s again came out of the U.S.A., the banks having forgotten
> the lessons of fifty years before. But, just as in the 1920s, so
> today: the rapid expansion and the way loans were used has much
> to do with the nature and the difficulties of the adjustment crisis.
> In 1976-78 lending never stopped, except to certain coun-
> tries....today the scenario of 1930 appears more appropriate.
> [Thorp and Whitehead (1987), p. 2]

The decline in the world commodity prices and the importance of the
capital account during these periods are also comparable. The role of the
United States today in the international financial system is compared to that
of Great Britain in the late 1920s. Thorp and Whitehead have contended:

> Since the breakdown of the Bretton Woods System, the U.S.A. has
> increasingly withdrawn from the responsibility of stabilizing the
> international economy, partly in response to domestic political
> pressures to become more inward-looking. In important respects,
> this mirrors the decline in the role of the U.K. in the first decades
> of the century. [Thorp and Whitehead (1987), p. 2]

The strategic role of the United States in the recent crisis makes it
imperative to evaluate the behavior of international capital movements to
developing countries by taking into account the developments within the
U.S. economy. In addition, the deadline for the application of the Basle
Accord Capital Adequacy Guidelines for financial institutions in the OECD
countries is fast approaching. Banks in the United States have to achieve
certain debt/equity ratios in their portfolios, among other things, by end-
1992 to avoid taxation. This has induced several U.S. banks to reduce their
LDC exposure very rapidly.[5] Developing country debt is primarily
denominated in U.S. dollars, a large proportion of which are variable interest rate loans. This makes these countries extremely vulnerable to real
interest rate fluctuations and any variation in the value of the dollar. For
example, as interest rates rose after 1979 and the U.S. dollar appreciated,
the debt service burden of developing countries (especially the HICs)
increased drastically. This rise in interest rates has had a different effect
on domestic debtors within the United States as compared to those abroad.
Thorp and Whitehead have quite rightly stated:

While the tightening of U.S. credit was meant to cut off domestic demand for credit within the U.S. by weak domestic borrowers, the end result of the policy hit the weakest borrowers outside the U.S.--and particularly the Latin American Nations, whose interest payments were of course not tax deductible, in contrast to those of most domestic debtors. [Thorp and Whitehead (1987), p. 3]

On the positive side, the expansionary monetary policy that followed immediately after 1982 to prevent the collapse of the U.S. banking system brought with it a growth in the U.S. economy. This spurt of economic growth, which followed between 1982-84, improved the trade balances of the HICs and somewhat alleviated their immediate debt-servicing difficulties. However, with the ongoing recessionary situation along with the emphasis on "inward-looking" policies within the United States, the increase in U.S. imports from these severely indebted countries is not expected to continue.

The international debt situation has not improved enough to restore the credit worthiness, and to bring about economic growth and development in the HICs. The debt overhang that continues to exist for these countries is an obstacle to their future growth prospects.[6] Even though debtor countries have been postponing their "day of reckoning" by rescheduling their outstanding debt or by obtaining more funds (often by "forced lending" by commercial banks under the auspices of the IMF and the World Bank), these have not been enough to prevent a substantial reduction in their per capita incomes and standard of living. Table 1.7 shows the decline in the rates of growth of real GDP, real GDP per capita, gross capital formation, increasing inflation rates, and deteriorating terms of trade for all LDCs and the "Baker 15" HICs (IMF definition). Compared to the average rate for 1972-81, all indicators show a deterioration in the conditions in the HICs in 1989-90. Terms of Trade for the LDCs, in general, and the HICs, in particular, have also become very unfavorable, especially since 1986 (Table 1.7). Pessimism over global prospects has made recovery of LDC credit worthiness less likely and creditors less willing to lend. Several HICs are considering default of their outstanding debt as a viable option for dealing with the debt crisis along with the other options (like rescheduling and rollover) that they have tried in vain, unless a significant amount of debt relief and softer terms on their foreign loans are granted by their creditors. It is this issue that will be addressed in the next section.

Table 1.7
The Highly Indebted Countries, 1972-90 (macroeconomic indicators)

	Average 1972-81	1982	1983	1984	1985	1986	1987	1988	1989	1990 *
REAL GDP (% rate of growth)										
All LDCs	5.0	2.1	2.2	4.1	3.9	4.0	3.9	4.2	3.0	2.2
HICs 1/	4.9	(0.5)	(2.9)	2.2	3.7	4.0	2.6	0.9	2.0	(0.2)
REAL GDP per capita (% rate of growth)										
All LDCs	2.3	(0.2)	(0.2)	1.8	1.7	1.7	1.4	2.1	0.9	0.4
HICs	2.2	(2.6)	(4.9)	(0.1)	1.6	1.8	0.4	(1.2)	(0.1)	(1.8)
GROSS CAPITAL FORMATION (% of GDP)										
All LDCs	-	24.9	23.6	23.8	23.5	23.5	23.3	23.4	22.7	22.9
HICs	-	22.0	17.8	16.3	16.9	17.8	19.0	19.1	17.9	18.4
CONSUMER PRICES 2/ (weighted avg. % rate)										
All LDCs	22.7	25.3	32.7	38.2	39.8	31.5	41.4	70.6	104.6	104.8
HICs	39.5	55.7	90.8	118.4	122.7	78.5	116.6	248.6	486.9	524.1
6 month US$ LIBOR(%)	-	13.6	9.9	11.3	8.6	6.8	7.3	8.1	9.3	8.4
TERMS OF TRADE (% rate of growth)										
All LDCs	7.0	(1.5)	(3.3)	1.6	(1.5)	(16.4)	1.8	(3.4)	2.3	(0.2)
HICs	4.9	(6.8)	(4.1)	4.6	(5.4)	(14.6)	-	(3.2)	0.8	(2.4)

Source: International Monetary Fund, World Economic Outlook, October 1990.

* Estimates

1. The highly indebted countries (HICs) include the 15 countries originally listed under the Baker Initiative in 1985. Namely, Argentina, Bolivia, Brazil, Chile, Colombia, Cote d'Ivoire, Ecuador, Mexico, Morocco, Nigeria, Peru, Philippines, Uruguay, Venezuela, and Yugoslavia.

2. The weights are the average U.S.$ GDP of each country over the preceding three years.

TO DEFAULT OR NOT TO DEFAULT--THAT IS THE QUESTION

Critical evaluation of the trends in international lending has revealed the seriousness of the LDC debt crisis. The crisis is not only a "financial crisis" in terms of the repayment capacity of these countries, but also a "development crisis" in terms of the inability to bring about economic growth and development in the presence of the large debt overhang in these developing countries. Under these circumstances, the creditors may demand full repayment of the total debt outstanding, or may choose to reschedule or roll over the debt. However, there is a distinct possibility that the demand for debt repayment by the creditor may motivate the debtor to repudiate the debt outstanding. The debtor country may express its inability or unwillingness to service its external debt liabilities in the short run.

Default of corporate debt will have different consequences from default of sovereign debt. If an indebted firm declares bankruptcy, its creditors have prior claim on its assets. It is not possible to transfer the "assets" of a country to its creditors in the event of a default on sovereign debt. The institutional arrangements under which international lending to developing countries takes place do not allow for collateral or seizure of assets upon default. In this context, Gerard Gennotte, Homi Kharas and Sayeed Sadeq (1987) have suggested three characteristics of assets of a country, as opposed to those of a firm. First, they represent the foreign exchange earning capacity of the country. This is associated with the country's expected future trade surpluses that could be generated given its resources. Second, they represent the cost that could be imposed on the country in the event of a repudiation. The defaulting country may be denied access to international financial markets and may face an embargo on future trade. Finally, country assets also include foreign exchange holdings abroad, which could be seized by the creditor in the event of a repudiation of the debt by the LDC debtor.[7]

The concentration of the debt, both on the creditors' side and the debtor's side, allows for the negotiation of a restructuring of existing obligations. Jeffrey Sachs and Daniel Cohen (1982) and Jonathan Eaton and Mark Gersovitz (1981) suggest that a default of debt repayments results from the strategic behavior of debtors. Given the possibility of repudiation at a later date, a country would be inclined to reschedule its debt service payments as long as possible. The creditor would prefer to reschedule the debt on the expectation that the debt would eventually be repaid once conditions in these developing countries became more favorable. Anytime these "presumptions" on the part of the debtors and creditors change, default becomes a viable option. Their conclusions are based on the crucial distinction between the "liquidity" position and the "solvency" situation of a debtor country.

Eaton and Gersovitz (1981) along with others, such as Sachs and Cohen (1982), Cline (1983), Sachs (1983), and Paul Krugman (1985), have evaluated the cost-benefit analysis carried out by debtors and creditors in deciding whether default is feasible or not. The debtor will decide to default if the perceived benefits are greater than the perceived costs. The benefit of defaulting will increase with the size of the country's outstanding debt. It is the fear of a large-scale default by several of the major debtors together that forces the creditors (mainly the commercial banks) to lend more. Krugman (1985) considers this "defensive lending" to be a rational response of the creditors to the threat of a repudiation by the major LDC debtors. Empirical evidence shows that the occurrence of a large-scale default by the HICs has been prevented by a combination of short-term and long-term rescheduling of interest and principal repayments. However, rescheduling and debt rollover have led to the increased indebtedness of these countries. Persistence of this situation over time will create a situation where the country just cannot repay its debt. Between 1987 and 1990, some other countries have, indeed, declared a moratorium on debt service payments to their external commercial bank creditors, whereas others have threatened to do so.[8] The fear of not being paid by some of the major LDC debtors, such as Brazil, Argentina, Venezuela, and the Philippines, among others, and pessimism about global prospects for improvement of the international debt situation contributed to the decision by commercial banks to increase their loan-loss reserves on loans to developing nations.[9] This action does not benefit the debtor nations. It merely illustrates the fact that creditors perceive a higher risk of loss on their loans to developing countries. However, the banks have also begun to realize that without granting some form of debt relief and some "new money" (if not individually, then as a group) in order for the debtors to reap the full benefits of their stringent economic adjustment measures, they have a very slim chance of being repaid by some of their LDC clients. These debtors have been obtaining a negative net transfer of funds from their external creditors and still continue to face a large debt overhang. In addition, external shocks, such as oil price fluctuations and increase in international interest rates, have made their situations even more precarious.

PROPOSALS SUGGESTED FOR DEALING
WITH THE DEBT CRISIS

The magnitude and complexity of the external indebtedness of the developing countries, in general, and the highly indebted Latin American countries, in particular, have initiated a considerable amount of research into the theoretical as well as the applied aspects of the International Debt Crisis. Three sets of issues have generally been examined:

- the causes of the crisis (especially the impact of external shocks on the debt situation of the developing country concerned);

- the effectiveness of the stabilization programs supported by the IMF and the World Bank in alleviating the "credit crunch" faced by these countries; and

- identifying ways out of the International Debt Crisis on a global basis "that range from theoretically feasible to quixotic" [*Finance and Development*, March 1987, p. 49].

The causes of the crisis that have been suggested include external shocks, such as the OPEC oil price hike, the rapid growth of the Eurocurrency markets during the period 1973-82, which made it possible for large amounts of funds to be channeled to the developing countries, high interest rates and recessionary conditions in the industrialized nations. There is considerable amount of divergence regarding the *primary* cause of the external debt crisis.

The solutions that have been suggested for dealing with the debt crisis have concentrated on the author's perception of the "primary" cause of the crisis. Anne Krueger (1986), Eduardo Weisner (1985b), Cline (1983, 1984, 1985), and Williamson (1985) attribute the major cause for the International Debt Crisis to external shocks, in general, with special reference to the OPEC oil price increase of 1973. Solis and Zedillo (1985) also turn to external shocks as the major factor explaining the increase in indebtedness of the HICs, but they emphasize the role of high interest rates in the international financial markets. Dornbusch (1985, 1986, 1987), Rudiger Dornbusch and Stanley Fischer (1984), and Chris Carvounis (1986) focus on poor performance of the countries concerned. Cline (1985) has also mentioned such factors as the global recession of 1981-82 and domestic factors (such as the overvalued exchange rate of the domestic currency and

low domestic exchange rates). Weisner has emphasized the effect of public
expenditure increases and domestic policies of the debtor governments on
external indebtedness, arguing that:

> The world recession and high real rates of interest in international
> markets aggravated the crisis, but I do not believe they created
> it....the debt crisis can be traced back to a fiscal disequilibrium,
> and ultimately to an unresolved political struggle between compet-
> ing groups that wanted to have a larger share of income. [Weisner
> (1985), p. 191]

Weisner contends that the lack of information on the part of commercial
bankers has often led to "overlending" in certain countries:

> International banks assumed that a sovereign risk was a small risk
> because public sectors normally do not default. As a result, they
> did not pay sufficient attention to the quality of economic policies
> in the debtor countries, nor did they worry about the economic
> feasibility of the investment projects they were directly or indirect-
> ly financing. [Weisner (1985), p. 192]

The difficulty faced by the international banks in directly monitoring the
use of the borrowed funds by the LDC debtors has made it imperative for
them to rely on the IMF to enforce its "conditionality" on the LDC
borrowers. Therefore, an agreement between the IMF and the LDC debtor
has been regarded as a prerequisite for any rescheduling of outstanding
loans by the private creditors.

The standard IMF prescription that is imposed on a borrower comprises
trade liberalization (which is facilitated by a devaluation of the domestic
currency, and liberalization of foreign exchange and import restrictions);
anti-inflationary measures (such as a reduction in government expenditure,
cutback in government subsidies, and freezing of real wages); a realignment
of wages and prices (especially of food and essential consumer goods) to
reflect its true scarcity value; and providing incentives to foreign investors.

Critical evaluation of the IMF austerity measures in the HICs has
shown that, although they have been successful in improving the short-run
trade balances of these countries, they have not facilitated the attainment of
sustained growth and development in these nations. It has been contended
by some that these IMF adjustment policies have been effective in
preventing a collapse of the international financial system but have been

destabilizing from the long-term point of view [Debt Crisis Network (1985)].

Carlos Diaz-Alejandro has quite appropriately summarized the international debt situation today by stating:

> It has become reasonably clear that the interaction of faulty domestic policies with the breakdown of normal international financial markets was the major trigger for the crisis, and that the cartelization by lenders and their governments of credit supplies has managed to save major international banks, but at the expense of growth in the debtor countries. [Diaz-Alejandro (1987), p. 9]

The need to bring about economic growth to allow reduction of the debt burden of the HICs is well understood. However, the importance of the structural characteristics of each of the countries concerned has not been appropriately incorporated into the analysis of the International Debt Crisis.

Numerous proposals have been put forward to alleviate the International Debt Crisis. None of these provide a comprehensive solution to the problem. Each proposal is aimed at treating the factor that, in the proponent's perception, is the primary cause of the crisis and can be divided into two broad groups: first, those that consider the *size* of the debt outstanding of the countries concerned, and second, those that change the *structure* of the existing debt.[10]

Changes in the Size of the Debt Outstanding

Proposals calling for new sources of financing for debtor countries are based on the premise that the maintenance of a continuous flow of resources to the HICs is essential in order for them to bring about sustained growth and to restore their credit worthiness in the international financial markets. These proposals include the formation of an Emergency Fund by the international organizations or the commercial banks themselves, an increase in the traditional lending by the IMF and the World Bank, and the formation of an Export Development Fund for the developing country exportables.

The question that follows from these proposals is whether these additional resources replace the involuntary lending that has occurred in the past when a country has faced repayment problems on its external debt. The question of burden-sharing also becomes relevant in this context (i.e., who benefits and who bears the cost of these additional funds). Also, once these additional funds are provided, they have to be used efficiently by the recipient countries. It may very well be that these additional resources could be used as a way of postponing adjustment by the debtor country concerned. The consequence of these proposals would inevitably be a further increase in the exposure of these international agencies (which may put their credit ratings at risk in the international financial markets).

Proposals calling for a guarantee of new commercial bank lending would unquestionably benefit the commercial banks but may be accompanied by the "moral hazard" problem. Bad loans would be made by the banks, because they would know that there would be a lender of last resort who would bail them out in case these loans threatened their financial viability. The proposals that have been suggested include the formation of a new international agency that would guarantee new commercial bank lending to developing countries. The guarantee could be provided by OECD governments or a multilateral development bank. The provision of "Credit Insurance" by the IMF and the World Bank has also been proposed, although this scheme may lead to an increase in the cost of borrowing for the debtor countries.

There are several proposals that suggest the creation of new financial instruments to enable increased resource flows into the HICs. Then U.S. treasury secretary, James Baker III proposed at the 1987 Annual Meetings of the IMF and the World Bank that the commercial banks develop a "menu of financing options" to increase lending to the HICs.[11] These instruments differ in their risk and term structure, and would accommodate different banks with different perceptions of the economic prospects of the HICs. These include futures contracts to hedge against interest rate and commodity price fluctuations; the use of zero-coupon bonds or floating rate consoles; introducing indexation clauses that link interest payment to the inflation rate; and new equity issues.

The Baker Initiative was, in fact, vigorously pursued during 1985-88 and results have been dismal. As reported by the World Bank:

> At the end of 1987 and in 1988 it became clear that the original Baker strategy had been unable to meet initial expectations concerning the contribution of commercial banks and the indebted countries were facing serious problems in keeping adjustment programs on track. The original Baker strategy underwent considerable modification during this period in response to both the behavior of commercial creditors and developments in debtor countries. [World Bank, "World Debt Tables, 1989-90," p. 13]

Changes in the Structure of Existing Debt

Forgiveness of some part of the debt burden of the indebted developing countries is a common component of most proposals that make changes in the terms and conditions of existing external debt obligations of the HICs. Not only is this easy to implement, but debt forgiveness also seems appropriate under the current circumstances, where the growth prospects of the HICs and the possibility of repayment of the loans to their international creditors in the near term are not very encouraging. Since 1982, the main type of debt relief has been in the form of comprehensive multi-year rescheduling of principal payments. This reduces the uncertainty about the amount of foreign exchange that will be available to the debtor countries concerned, thereby allowing for medium-term planning of resource allocation in these economies.

Rescheduling of principal amortization has been preferred by the U.S. commercial banks under the existing banking regulations. This minimizes the adverse effect on their balance sheets (and, hence, profits and dividends paid out to their shareholders). Other proposals that have been suggested in this category include lower interest rates on outstanding debt, linking of debt repayment to export earnings, debt-equity swaps, spreading out of maturities for a longer period of time, and a partial write-off or moratorium of the total debt outstanding in the HICs.

The proposal of charging lower interest rates on the outstanding debt of the HICs is based on the premise that its current market value is below its nominal value. The current market value can be calculated by looking at the secondary market for developing country debt (the extent of this market is still quite limited). According to this proposal, it would be appropriate, under these circumstances, to reduce interest payments in proportion to the adjustment made to the nominal value of the debt outstanding. A reduction in the interest charged on developing country debt outstanding would make the international banks incur losses and reduce the availability of new loans to the troubled HICs because of the fear of further downward adjustment of the interest rate by these countries.

By linking debt repayment to export earnings, there would be a shift in the risk (arising from adverse conditions in the world market for the exportables of the highly indebted country) away from the debtor nation towards the creditor banks. The argument in favor of this proposal is that banks are much more competent in hedging against fluctuations in commodity prices as compared to the debtor countries. However, a consequence of this may be that the commercial banks may raise the cost of funds to the debtors for carrying this additional risk.

Debt-equity swaps are being used by several countries (e.g., Argentina, Bolivia, Brazil, Chile, Côte d'Ivoire, Ecuador, Mexico, Nigeria, the Philippines, Turkey, Venezuela, and Yugoslavia), but the volume of trading of these instruments continues to be quite small.[12] In 1986, less than 1 percent of the external debt of developing countries was traded in these secondary markets.[13] However, this market is expanding and becoming more organized. Debt-equity swaps have the ability to attract direct foreign investment as well as flight capital, since they are available to residents as well as nonresidents of the debtor country with foreign currency holdings abroad. The issue of the *transfer price* (i.e., the value at which one dollar of debt will be exchanged in the market) and the problem of selecting the enterprises that would allow equity participation under this scheme become important in this context. The debtor country would prefer to sell equity of the least economically viable enterprises, whereas the creditors would prefer to buy equity of the best enterprises. The issue of foreign ownership of domestic assets has political connotations, and negotiations on the intricacies of the debt conversion scheme often tend to be prolonged.

Proposals that call for a bailout of the commercial banks include the formation of a Rediscount Facility for commercial bank loans to developing countries by Central Banks or Export Credit Agencies of industrial countries; the transfer of claims to the IMF/World Bank for refunding existing debt; and expansion of the secondary market for developing country debt. It is proposed that a third party (e.g., a newly created international organization) would provide the highly indebted country relief by converting short-term and medium-term floating rate loans to long-term assets (such as exchange participation notes, tieing debt service to the country's export earnings, variable maturity consoles, discounted zero-coupon bonds). The question that is crucial in this context regards the financing of this new Rediscount Facility. The *amount* of subsidy given to the debtor country also has to be determined. The expansion of the secondary market for developing country debt would help establish this market value for the debt outstanding of each country. The secondary market could also allow countries with an adequate stock of international reserves to purchase and retire its own debt at a discount.

Critics of these proposals contend that the bailout of commercial banks would lead to a "moral hazard" problem, whereby commercial banks would become reckless in their future lending to developing countries. Some have argued that it was this lack of discipline on the part of the commercial banks that brought about the International Debt Crisis in the first place.[14]

Other proposals that have been put forward recommend adjustment through growth of the OECD countries, continuation of what has been done in the past (i.e. restructuring, rollover and IMF austerity programs) and increasing supervision of commercial bank lending to developing countries by the IMF and the Central Banks. It is believed that the stability of the international financial system will be improved by these long-term structural reforms.

The merits of each of these proposals will depend on the specific country concerned. A viable solution to the international debt crisis will, indeed, contain a combination of these above-mentioned proposals and a few new ones. The International Debt Crisis is yet to be resolved.

THE DEBT OVERHANG AND A GROWTH-ORIENTED DEBT REDUCTION STRATEGY

In August 1982, Mexico brought the Intentional Debt Crisis to the forefront by abruptly declaring a moratorium on the debt service payments, which were due during the remainder of 1982 and in 1983. By the end of the following year, forty-two countries were behind in their debt service payments.[15]

The debt crisis was treated as a "financial crisis," i.e., it posed a threat to the international financial system, since a collapse of the major international banks would have adverse effects on both the industrialized countries as well as the LDC debtors. It was believed that the highly indebted debtor countries were facing a "liquidity" problem, and that because of an expected decline in interest rates in the international financial markets, renewed growth in the industrialized nations, an improvement in world trade in favor of the developing nations (i.e., the Terms of Trade of developing countries were expected to improve), and new financing in the interim period in order to support the austerity measures being carried out by the debtor countries, the crisis would be resolved. The financial collapse would be averted, and the highly indebted developing countries would, once again, become creditworthy in the international financial markets.

The policies that were implemented during this first phase of the debt crisis were, indeed, successful in averting a collapse in the international financial system. During 1982-83, numerous debt restructuring and financial packages were negotiated between the creditors and the HICs with the objective of buying time until the economic conditions in these countries improved.[16] The commercial banks used this time to strengthen their portfolios, reduce their exposure to developing countries, and make themselves less susceptible to losses on their loans to developing countries.

The assumptions on the basis of which policies were prescribed in the first phase of the debt crisis have not materialized. The involuntary lending by the commercial banks that took place between 1983-86 has led to the existence of a debt overhang in the highly indebted Latin American countries that will make it difficult for them to bring about growth and improve their credit worthiness in the international financial markets. Concerning the past debt management policies, it has been contended that "while forestalling the collapse of the entire financial system, this management has been anti-developmental, destabilizing and inequitable in a fashion that will have serious long-term consequences" [Debt Crisis Network (1985), p. 14]. Given the magnitudes involved and the future growth prospects of the debtor countries along with the expected increase in debt service payments in the near future in the presence of a debt overhang, we have entered the second phase of the International Debt Crisis where a short-term solution will not be feasible anymore.

At this juncture, it is necessary to re-evaluate the situation of the HICs with respect to the present structure of their financial systems as well as changed conditions in the international financial system. The reassessment of the debt crisis has to be conducted with the premise that it is not only a "financial crisis," but also a "development crisis." In this context, the overall economic and institutional characteristics of each individual country's financial system become vital to the analysis. Graham Bird has quite rightly stated that "debt is but one aspect of a much broader problem of economic management and should not be viewed in isolation" [Bird (1985), p. 51]. A proper reassessment of the situation requires an understanding of the changes that have occurred over time in the socio-economic structure of the HIC under consideration. Diaz-Alejandro has stated in this context:

> It would be difficult to argue that the ten relatively good perform-
> ers suddenly became, during the early 1980s, more corrupt, more
> hostile to foreign investors and more biased against exports. It is
> also implausible that countries whose policies could not have been
> that atrocious for two decades would, in a fit of collective mania,
> all start blatantly mismanaging their affairs during the early 1980s.
> [Diaz-Alejandro (1987), p. 10]

Unlike the previous decade, in the 1980s it was crucial to realize the link between the rise in interest rates in the international financial markets and the *automatic* increase in the external debt burden on the HIC concerned. Conventional adjustment measures had become less effective as a result of this "interest rate effect." More specifically, the balance of payments disequilibrium of the debtor country deteriorated further because of this rise in interest payments. Rising debt service payments implied that imports had to be reduced further and export earnings increased. With the limited resources at the disposal of the HIC concerned, if it chooses to service its debt, it will have to reduce domestic aggregate demand, especially domestic investment. When this is combined with a situation of persistent inflation (as is true for the highly indebted Latin American countries), the crisis situation is aggravated.

Under an inflationary environment, a part of the interest payment on external debt is, what should have been, principal amortization. Also, as Thorp and Whitehead have pointed out, there may be a distortion in policy goals as interest payments on external debt flow *directly* out of the economy.[17] If the external debt of a country accrues primarily to the public sector (as in Mexico), then the Government's budget deficit will *include* interest payments on external debt and expenditure on strategic imports by the public sector enterprises. Therefore, an adjustment policy that calls for a general reduction in *domestic* economic activity will be inappropriate if it ignores this interest rate effect on the external debt and the effect of changes in the prices of imports of the public sector (which is beyond their control) on the Government's budget deficit. The transmission mechanism, which suggests that a large fiscal deficit causes excess demand in the *domestic* economy, which, in turn, leads to inflationary pressures and a balance of payments disequilibrium, is inappropriate here. Under these circumstances, inflationary pressure on the domestic economy will emerge from the exchange rate (i.e., the external disequilibrium). Any meaningful adjustment efforts on the part of this inflation-ridden, HIC should incorporate these characteristics. The internal and external disequilibrium will have to be tackled *simultaneously*.

The concept of inertial inflation has also become pertinent in the current situation. When inflation becomes persistent for a long time, the increase in prices in any given time will be strongly be influenced by the behavior of prices in the past. In Brazil, this inertial inflation resulted from the formal indexation that was done.[18] Inertial inflation could also result from policy responses and expectations of the private sector emerging from the behavior of four crucial economic variables: the exchange rate, domestic interest rate, prices of goods produced in the "controlled" sector, and the wage rate. This does not require any kind of formal indexation. The capital flight problem is closely linked to the expectations of the private sector about these four variables. Mexico is a perfect candidate for analysis of this kind of *informal* indexation and its consequences on the external debt burden of the country. In this context, Thorp and Whitehead have stated:

> As inertial inflation becomes entrenched, so inflation becomes less responsive to demand, and therefore to the typical adjustment package used. This, together with the significance of increased interest burden goes far to explaining the diminishing returns to conventional adjustment measures and the growing appeal of so-called "heterodox shocks" such as the Plan Austral adopted in Argentina in mid-1985 and the Cruzado Plan in Brazil in early 1986. [Thorp and Whitehead (1987), pp. 6]

Another development that needs to be addressed is the changing relationship between the private sector and the Government under these conditions of persistent inflation and pessimistic growth prospects for the Latin American HICs. The private sector tries to acquire subsidies from the Government and guarantees from their major customers--the public sector enterprises--in an endeavor to "live with inflation." The behavior of the public sector provides a signal to the private sector about their perception of the future course of the economy. More specifically, private net investment in the economy follows public net investment with a lag.

We have now entered the 1990s: The debt overhang problem has become acute; private sector developments, in general, and private investment, in particular, has been adversely affected in the recent past. The Debt-Laffer Curve has to be tackled head on. Perhaps, with a growth-oriented debt reduction strategy. In this endeavor, we will now examine the case of the "Golden Child" of the international financial community--Mexico--which after almost a decade of stringent adjustment measures is no better off than it was before the 1982 crisis (in terms of its macroeconomic indicators for growth and development).

SUMMARY AND CONCLUSIONS

The objective of this chapter is to provide an overview of the trends in external indebtedness of the developing countries, in general, and those in Latin America, in particular. The general characteristics of the debt problem are presented in some detail along with a survey of the proposals that have been recommended in the ongoing endeavor to solve the International Debt Crisis.

Empirical evidence clearly indicates the rapid increase in external indebtedness of the developing countries in terms of both rates of growth as well as levels of external debt outstanding. The largest amount of external borrowing from official as well as private sources has been directed towards the middle-income countries. The burden of external debt is quite unequal across the developing countries. On the one hand, there are a few large debtors that are causing great concern to the international financial community (especially the large money center banks); on the other are those countries that include the poorest nations in the world and that are at the mercy of the developments in the international financial system. A regional concentration can also be gleaned with respect to the HICs. Twelve of the nineteen SIMICs (World Bank definition) are in Latin America. Most of the debt outstanding of these countries has been obtained from private sources. These loans primarily charge a variable interest rate (usually a markup over LIBOR) that is payable in U.S. dollars. This makes these countries extremely vulnerable to real interest rate fluctuations and any variation in the value of the U.S. dollar. There exists a concentration of lenders as well, with the number of private creditors who have significant exposure to developing countries being very small (e.g., the nine largest money center banks in the United States).

The international debt situation has not improved enough to restore the credit worthiness and to bring about economic growth and development in the SIMICs. Compared to the year 1980, all basic economic indicators show a deterioration in the conditions in these countries in 1989. Pessimism over global prospects has made recovery of LDC credit worthiness less likely and creditors less willing to lend. The worsening debt situation is quite apparent from the rising debt service ratios in spite of the limited increase in exposure of commercial banks to developing countries.

Critical evaluation of the trends in international lending has revealed the seriousness of the LDC debt crisis. The crisis is not only a "financial crisis" in terms of the repayment capacity of these countries, but also a "development crisis" in terms of the inability to bring about economic growth and development in the presence of the large debt overhang in these developing countries.

The magnitude and complexity of the external indebtedness of the developing countries, in general, and the severely indebted Latin American countries, in particular, have initiated a considerable amount of research into the theoretical as well as the applied aspects of the International Debt Crisis.

Numerous proposals have been put forward to alleviate the International Debt Crisis. None of these provides a comprehensive solution to the

problem. Each proposal is aimed at treating the factor that, in the proponent's perception, is the primary cause of the crisis. The proposals that
have been suggested for dealing with the International Debt Crisis can be
divided into two broad groups: first, those that consider the *size* of the debt
outstanding of the countries concerned, and second, those that change the
structure of the existing debt.

During the first phase of the International Debt Crisis, which began
after Mexico declared a moratorium on its debt service payments in August
1982, it was believed that the HICs were facing a "liquidity" problem rather
than an "insolvency" problem that was of a temporary nature. During
1982-83, numerous debt restructuring and financial packages were negotiated between the creditors and the HICs with the objective of buying time
until the economic conditions in these countries improved. The assumptions
on the basis of which policies were prescribed in the first phase of the debt
crisis have not materialized. The involuntary lending by the commercial
banks that took place between 1983-86 has led to the existence of a debt
overhang in the highly indebted Latin American countries that will make it
difficult for them to bring about growth and improve their credit worthiness
in the international financial markets.

The international debt situation has not improved enough to restore the
credit worthiness, and to bring about economic growth and development in
the SIMICs. The debt overhang that continues to exist in these countries
is an obstacle to their future growth prospects. Even though debtor
countries have been postponing their "day of reckoning" by rescheduling
their outstanding debt or by obtaining more funds (often by "forced lending"
by commercial banks under the auspices of the IMF and the World Bank),
these have not been enough to prevent a substantial reduction in their per
capita incomes and standard of living.

A reassessment on a country-by-country basis is necessary in light of
the changes that have occurred over time in the socioeconomic structure of
the HIC under consideration and the developments in the international
financial system. The reassessment of the debt crisis has to be conducted
with the premise that it is not only a "financial crisis," but also a "development crisis." In this context, the overall economic and institutional
characteristics of each individual country's financial system become vital to
the analysis. It is with this in mind that an evaluation of the Mexican
economy will be carried out for the period 1973-89 in the following
chapters.

NOTES

1. These countries, which are facing severe debt-servicing difficulties, are Argentina, Bolivia, Brazil, Chile, Colombia, Costa Rica, Cote d'Ivoire, Ecuador, Jamaica, Mexico, Morocco, Nigeria, Peru, Philippines, Uruguay, Venezuela, and Yugoslavia. These consist of the "Baker 15" highly indebted middle-income countries (as classified by the IMF) plus Costa Rica and Jamaica.

2. Net transfers *equals* Disbursements *minus* Total debt service, where debt service consists of repayments of the principal and interest payments.

3. Refer to Graham Bird (1985) for details on each of the alternative debt indicators used in the context of understanding the International Debt Crisis.

4. This view is shared by Lorie Tarshis (1984), who calls for a reform in the international monetary system so as to increase the degree of international cooperation among debtors and creditors in the ongoing endeavor to solve the International Debt Crisis.

5. See Johnathan Hay and Michel Bouchet, (1989) "The Tax Accounting and Regulatory Treatment of Sovereign Debt," (Mimeo), Washington, D.C.: World Bank, for details.

6. Refer to Krueger (1986) and Dornbusch (1986) for a description of the consequences of a large debt overhang on the future growth and debt repayment capacity of the HICs.

7. This, in fact, occurred in the case of Ecuador in May 1989, when one creditor bank invoked a cross default clause to accelerate a trade financing facility to Ecuador and then applied credit balances standing in the accounts of the Central Bank to satisfy amounts due under the accelerated trade financing.

8. On February 20, 1987, Brazil declared an indefinite moratorium on interest payments on its $68 billion medium- and long-term debt outstanding to private creditors.

9. In May 1987, Citicorp raised its provisions against potential losses on its portfolio of loans to developing countries to $3 billion. They were followed by most major banks in Great Britain, Canada and the United States.

10. See Appendix A for a summary of the proposals for dealing with the International Debt Crisis. Cline (1983) has classified the proposals on the basis of who the direct beneficiaries of the proposal are. Some proponents (e.g., Debt Crisis Network, 1985) have classified the proposals on the basis of whether they are consistent with the existing international financial system or whether they require a reform in the present system.

Although these alternative classifications are conceptually clear, it is important to realize that there could be benefits accruing to both debtors and creditors from the same proposal, for example, if commercial bank lending to developing countries is guaranteed by an external agency and this results in an increased amount of new lending to the HICs. Also, there is an interdependence among different proposals or they may overlap.

11. See World Bank, "World Debt Tables," 1987-88 edition, p. xvi, Box 3 for a more detailed description of the instruments included in the menu of financing options for commercial banks. Also refer to Fred Bergsten, William Cline, and John Williamson (1985) Table 2.1, pp. 60-66 for a summary of the effects of alternative proposals.

12. See World Bank, "World Development Report," 1987, pp. 22, Box 2.2 for details on how debt-equity swaps function.

13. World Bank, "World Development Report," 1987, p. 22.

14. For details on specific debt relief proposals (e.g., those postulated by Lever, Kenen, Rohatyn, Baker, Bradley, Herrhausen, LaFalce, Sachs), see World Bank, "World Debt Tables," 1987-88, p. xviii.

15. Debt Crisis Network (1985), p. 7.

16. See "Recent Multilateral Debt Restructurings with Official and Bank Creditors," *IMF Occasional Paper* No. 25, December 1983 and "Recent Developments in External Debt Restructuring," *IMF Occasional Paper* No. 40, October 1985 for details on debt restructuring and financial packages negotiated between 1978-85.

17. See Thorp and Whitehead (1987).

18. See Werner Baer, "The Resurgence of Inflation in Brazil, 1974-86," L. Bresser Pereira, "Inertial Inflation and the Cruzado Plan,"; Donald Coes, "Inertial Inflation and the Cruzado Plan: Discussion," and P. D. McNelis, "Indexation, Exchange Rate Policy and Inflationary Feedback Effects in Latin America," all in *World Development*, Vol. 15, No. 7, July 1987 in this context.

2

Developments in Mexico Until 1982:
The Seeds of the Crisis Are Sown

The evaluation of the basic characteristics of the Debt Problem of the highly indebted countries that was presented in the previous chapter clearly suggests that productive investment and economic growth are necessary prerequisites for enabling these countries to return to credit worthiness in the financial markets. In addition, the need to proceed with the ongoing endeavor to solve the debt crisis on a *case-by-case* basis is quite apparent. A critical evaluation of each case would provide lessons towards achieving a better understanding of the debt situation, from which the pieces of the puzzle could be put together in an organized manner and a viable solution attained. It is the objective of this book to evaluate the role of and developments in one of the most important highly indebted countries of the world--Mexico--in order to use the stylized facts of this country to move a step closer to providing a viable solution to the debt-servicing difficulties of a country faced with a large debt overhang, which is an impediment to increasing investment and growth and, eventually, its return to the voluntary capital markets. This reassessment of the debt crisis has to be conducted in light of the changes that have occurred over time in the socioeconomic structure of the highly indebted country in question. As Graham Bird has contended, "Debt is but one aspect of a much broader problem of economic management and should not be viewed in isolation" [Bird (1985), p. 51].

Mexico has been a crucial player in the historical evolution of the debt crisis. It was Mexico that brought the International Debt Crisis to the forefront in August 1982, when it abruptly proposed an indefinite suspension of the payments of principal that were due during the remainder of 1982 and in 1983 to all creditors, as well as interest payments, to its

private creditors.   At that time, Mexico had the second largest gross
external debt burden in Latin America (after Brazil). In this context,
Menachem Katz (1989) has stated that:

> Although Mexico was not the first developing country faced with
> default, it was the first one in which the international banking
> system had a great deal at stake. The "Mexican Debt Crisis" came
> as a surprise not only to the international banking system, to whom
> Mexico had a great deal of exposure, but also to the industrial
> countries, particularly the U.S. No less surprised were the
> Mexicans, for their economy was in the midst of an unprecedented
> boom following the discovery of massive oil reserves.   [Katz
> (1989), p. 369]

Fourteen countries in Latin America followed in Mexico's footsteps
within the next few months and declared their inability to meet their
contractual debt service obligations. Between 1982 and 1987, Mexico had
experienced periods of crisis, of heavy doses of IMF-type stabilization programs, and periods in which Mexico was the "shining star" of the Baker
Plan.

Mexico has been the initiator of some very innovative schemes in
dealing with the debt crisis.   In September 1986, Mexico was the first
debtor nation to negotiate $7.7 billion in additional loans from commercial
banks at an interest rate spread of only 13/16th percentage points over the
London Interbank Offer Rate (LIBOR), which was the lowest interest rate
granted by commercial banks to any highly indebted country at the time.
What also made this "Mexican rescue package" unique was the built-in
"growth-trigger mechanism," wherein additional funds would automatically
become available to Mexico in the event of a sharp decline in the price of
oil or if economic growth was below its targeted level in early 1987.
Mexico has been successful in extracting concessions from its official and
private creditors via long negotiations. In February 1988, Mexico initiated
the Mexico-J. P. Morgan debt conversion scheme (the Aztec Bond), which
was another attempt to redefine the conventional guidelines of debt
management by making the concept of debt reduction a reality. More recently, in September 1989, Mexico became the first candidate to receive
resources from the multilateral agencies in order to reduce its public and
publicly guaranteed debt outstanding and disbursed from commercial bank
creditors. This was achieved under a comprehensive debt and debt service
reduction (DDSR) agreement which it negotiated with the banks under the
auspices of the "Brady Initiative." All eyes are on Mexico even today to

learn from its experience and, more often than not, follow in its footsteps in dealing with a country's debt-servicing difficulties. In the 1990s, Mexico has entered the international financial markets once again.

In this chapter, the Mexican experience during the first phase of the debt crisis (1973-82) is reviewed. The interaction between domestic fiscal, monetary and exchange rate policies of the Government and expectational changes in the perceptions of the private investors and savers is examined. Budget deficits, inflation, and capital flight were instrumental in leaving Mexico with a large debt overhang. The question that becomes important from a long-term perspective is the extent to which continuing fiscal problems and the debt overhang contributed to the decline in investment and growth in the Mexican economy. The interaction between domestic macroeconomic performance and external constraints is highlighted in this context. It would be interesting to follow the developments in Mexico during the 1973-82 period to determine how the country could have found itself in a severe economic crisis only six years after having overcome (mainly because of its good fortune of discovering large oil reserves) a previous economic crisis.

This study begins with 1973, because this year was a turning point in Mexico's history of external borrowing. In the two decades prior to the 1970s the amount of foreign borrowing by Mexico had been moderate. Budget deficits were at levels that could be viable on the basis of Mexico's domestic resources and the current account of the balance of payments at the time. Only $200 million per year, on average, in foreign loans flowed into Mexico during this entire period. In 1973, the net flow of foreign public debt was more than $1.6 billion. Thereafter, the level of external public debt continued to grow (as shown in Table 2.1). Small budget deficits and price stability were a thing of the past.

Although the period of study begins in 1973, a brief description of the historical evaluation of the external indebtedness of Mexico prior to this period is provided. This would make it possible to understand "initial conditions" that existed in the Mexican economy on the eve of the period under consideration.

The 1973-82 period, which was characterized by large budget deficits, inflation, and increased borrowing from abroad, can itself be broken up into two subperiods: (i) 1973-76, the pre-oil period, and (ii) 1977-82, after the oil boom until August 1982, when Mexico declared a moratorium on debt service payments to its commercial bank creditors. This was followed by a suspension of voluntary lending from private sources abroad, and a period of fiscal retrenchment and stringent adjustment measures. The post-1982 period will be discussed in the following chapter.

Table 2.1
External Debt of Mexican Public Sector, 1950-82
(Billions of U.S. Dollars)

Year	Total External Debt	% Change from Prev. Year
1950	0.11	
1951	0.12	12.5%
1952	0.16	31.3%
1953	0.19	18.9%
1954	0.23	21.3%
1955	0.40	77.8%
1956	0.44	10.5%
1957	0.51	15.9%
1958	0.60	17.5%
1959	0.65	7.7%
1960	0.81	25.3%
1961	0.98	20.9%
1962	1.13	14.6%
1963	1.32	16.8%
1964	1.72	31.0%
1965	1.81	4.9%
1966	1.89	4.3%
1967	2.18	15.3%
1968	2.48	14.1%
1969	2.94	18.6%
1970	4.26	44.8%
1971	4.55	6.6%
1972	5.06	11.4%
1973	7.07	39.6%
1974	9.98	41.1%
1975	14.27	43.0%
1976	19.43	36.2%
1977	22.91	17.9%
1978	26.26	14.6%
1979	29.76	13.3%
1980	33.81	13.6%
1981	52.96	56.6%
1982	59.73	12.8%

Source: Direcion General de Planeacion Hacendaria, SHCP, Mexico, D.F.

Chart 2.1
Public Sector External Debt, 1950-82

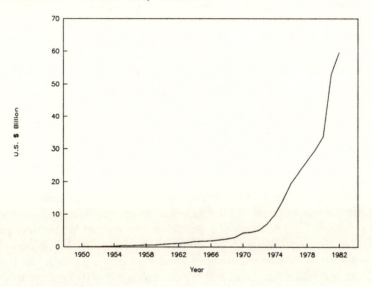

Chart 2.2
Debt Owed to Foreign Banks, 1976-83

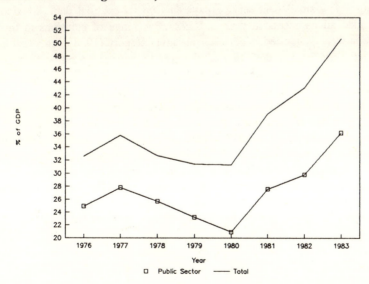

THE EARLY YEARS

Although Mexico has been given the dubious distinction of bringing the International Debt Crisis to the forefront in 1982, it was not the first time this nation faced repayment problems on its external debt.

In 1914, under the presidency of Victoriano Huerta, Mexico had suspended interest payments on all outstanding external debt. It was not until the "Lamont-de la Huerta Accord" of 1922 that Mexico resumed the partial repayment of its debt service obligations. However, this accord was again suspended in June 1924 because of the "costly rebellion and sharply declining revenues from the oil production and oil export taxes" [Bodayla (1982), p. 462]. In 1925, Mexico's external debt was rescheduled under the auspices of the "Lamont-Pani Agreement." Debt service payments were deferred and stretched out over an eight year period. In 1927, Mexico was again faced with difficulties in meeting its debt service obligations to its external creditors. The Mexican government under President Plutarco Elias Calles attributed these payment difficulties primarily to the decline in oil revenues. It was believed that the American petroleum firms had reduced their production in retaliation of a petroleum law enacted at that time (in 1925) that they considered to be confiscatory. By 1928, Mexico owed $26.5 million to its external creditors [Bodayla (1982), p. 464]. At this time, the Mexican government had begun implementing its agrarian land-reform measures along with increases in expenditure on infrastructure projects to improve education and public works. These provided a drain on its financial resources in the face of declining revenues at the time. After making a few small debt service payments on its external debt, Mexico suspended all payments in year end 1927. A range of solutions to this problem were suggested. The Sterret-Davis Report (1928) suggested a comprehensive plan to deal with *all* the creditors at one go rather than on a bilateral basis, whereas the McBride Recommendations (1928) suggested a partial debt write-off by the major creditors of Mexico.[1]

The stock of Mexico's external debt outstanding on the eve of World War II consisted of the arrears of debts contracted in the nineteenth century and debts contracted up to 1913, which were used to finance the Mexican Revolution, the debt of the Mexican railways, the payments that had to be made to foreigners whose land had been expropriated in conjunction with the agrarian reforms, claims by foreign shareholders of the petroleum firms that had been nationalized, external debt of the Mexican states, and the unpaid portion of debt service payments accruing between 1923 and 1927.[2]

After continuous negotiations between Mexico and its creditors, the Suarez-Lamont Agreement was reached in 1942, wherein a partial debt write-off of the Mexican foreign debt reduced the claims of foreigners on Mexico considerably.[3]

IMPORT SUBSTITUTION INDUSTRIALIZATION, 1947-70

Mexico embarked on an import-substitution industrialization (ISI) strategy of development shortly after World War II. In this context, Eliana Cardoso and Santiago Levy have contended that:

As with many other Latin American countries, industrialization in Mexico was partly a choice of policy makers and partly the result of changing world conditions. World War II increased the demand for primary products in the world market and reduced the supply of manufactured goods to the developing countries. Mexican entrepreneurs faced increasing profits in a growing and protected domestic market. By the early 1950s, industrialization had become an explicit policy based on the influential thinking of Raul Prebisch and the Economic Commission for Latin America. [Cardoso and Levy (1988), p. 355].

Tariffs and import licensing were introduced in order to protect domestic producers from international competition. Other ISI policies included the granting of accelerated depreciation for fixed investment and incentives for the purchase of capital goods. Key inputs produced by the Mexican public sector (such as electricity and fuel) were made available to domestic firms at subsidized prices. During this period, the structure of relative prices was such that it promoted the adoption of capital-intensive methods of production in Mexico. The incentive system in Mexico at that time was such that exports were declining, which, in conjunction with increased imports of crucial intermediate and capital goods, brought about large trade deficits. Initially, import substitution policies were implemented in the consumer goods industries, such as textiles and chemicals, and later spread to consumer durables, such as appliances, automobiles, and electronic goods (in which, however, multinationals played a dominant role).[4]

Between 1945 and 1955, growth was erratic and prices unstable. Growth was induced through large budget deficits and investment in excess of savings. The current account deficit in the balance of payments that

Table 2.2
Inflation and Growth in Mexico, 1945-55

Year	Rates of Growth (%)	
	GDP	CPI
1945	2.7	7.4
1946	5.9	24.7
1947	3.7	11.9
1948	4.5	6.4
1949	6.0	5.0
1950	9.4	6.7
1951	7.3	13.6
1952	4.1	14.1
1953	0.4	-0.9
1954	10.5	4.8
1955	8.7	13.8

Source: Cardoso and Levy (1988), p. 350, Table 16.2

followed was counteracted by a devaluation of the peso that, in turn, fueled inflation.

For the next fifteen years (1955-70), the Mexican government embarked on a period of "Stabilizing Development." This period was characterized by a *fixed* nominal exchange rate that was supported by external borrowing. ISI policies were continued via tariffs and import licensing. Incentives were given to encourage reinvestment of profits by firms and savings by individuals. The Central Bank used reserve requirements of financial intermediaries not only as a tool of monetary policy, but as a way of financing the public sector deficit. The Banco de Mexico set reserve requirements as a technique to absorb government debt and provide compulsory loans to the Government. Loepoldo Solis had found that the weighted average of legal reserves was more than 40 percent during this period of Stabilizing Development [Weintraub (1981) p. 278]. In this way, it affected the allocation of credit between the public and private sectors in Mexico.

External borrowing from commercial banks was mainly in the form of:

- short-term trade financing and interbank lines of credit,
- working capital and investment for multinational corporations operating in Mexico, and
- funds for the operations of multinational banks that were allowed to open branches in Mexico [Hakim (1985) p. 17].

The pursuit of import-substitution policies, along with a fixed nominal exchange rate regime, led to an incentive system in the Mexican economy that was biased against the agricultural sector and labor-intensive techniques of production. Agricultural output declined, and Mexico became a net importer of basic food items. The antiexport bias had induced the slowing down of the growth of nontraditional exports. Francisco Gil Diaz (1985a) has contended that public investment as a share of GDP was kept low as a matter of policy under this "Stabilizing Development" regime (which required that low ratios of Government budget deficits to GDP be maintained). As a result, it was the investment by the government in the agricultural and education sectors that was curtailed. Public investment that took place at this time was devoted to increasing the size of the industrial sector of Mexico, but this was carried out at the expense of social infrastructure creation. Also, the projects that were undertaken could not be solely financed by domestic resources. In effect, the subsidization of the industrial sector of Mexico was partly financed by external borrowing.[5]

Rosario Green (1976) estimated the sectoral distribution of external public debt during this period of "Stabilizing Development" and showed that about 2/3 of the finances obtained from external sources was directed towards the development of industry, transportation, electrification, and activities that would primarily benefit the manufacturing sector (see Table 2.3).

The pursuit of a path of ISI did, however, lead to spectacular results in terms of macroeconomic performance with high growth rates of real GDP (6 percent per year on average, for the entire period) and low rates of inflation (about 3.8 percent per annum). The protectionist policies in trade led to falling exports as a share of GDP. With the increase of "strategic" imports (needed for maintaining previously imported capital goods), the trade deficit began to increase drastically.

The fixed nominal exchange rate policy that was being followed by the Government at this time made matters worse (i.e., the real exchange rate appreciated continuously during the entire period). Gil Diaz (1984) has shown that between 1955 and 1975 there was a continuous appreciation in the "effective real exchange rate." In arriving at an estimate of this rate, Gil Diaz used the weighted average of the wholesale prices (converted to pesos) of the twenty-one countries that accounted for 95 percent of Mexico's total trade at the time.[6]

On the whole, during the three decades after 1940, the Mexican economy experienced an average growth rate of 6 percent per annum, inflation was under control, and the private sector showed rapid development (especially steel, automobiles, textiles, tourism, and the cultivation of fruits and vegetables in the irrigated areas of Mexico). [Kraft (1984), p. 31]. ISI policies, which were pursued prior to 1970, were instrumental in rapidly developing the manufacturing sector of Mexico (Table 2.4). However, protection from foreign competition and production by firms for the captive domestic markets prevented industry from becoming efficient enough to compete abroad. The primary goods sector was penalized, and virtually all sectors of the economy become dependent on fiscal incentives, such as subsidized input prices, preferential credit, and a procurement policy of the public sector wherein it purchased only Mexican goods.

During the strategy of "Desarollo Estabilizador"[7] (1955-70), the public sector deficit was kept at moderate levels and was financed through the Mexican banking system. The prevailing taxation policies at that time were quite lenient, with low rates of taxation of corporate profits and generous subsidies and transfers to the private sector. These policies, in conjunction with the pre-existing disparity in the distribution of productive assets, further aggravated the inequality in income distribution in Mexico.

Table 2.3
Sectoral Distribution of External Borrowing of the Mexican Public Sector, 1958-70

Sector	Lopez Mateos (1958-64)	Diaz Ordaz (1965-70)
	(Percent of total external funds available)	
Transport	27.0	21.9
Electrification	22.0	23.8
Industry	12.0	12.0
Agriculture	11.0	12.0
Irrigation Works	8.3	13.5
Drinking Water	1.3	1.5
Housing	7.2	-
Higher Education	0.2	0.3
Other	11.0	15.0
Total	100.0	100.0

Source: Green, Rosario (1976), pp. 141, 165, 185.

Table 2.4
Sectoral Growth Rates, 1950-75

	Real rates of growth		(1960 = 100)
	1950-65	1965-70	1970-75
	(Percent)		
Gross Domestic Product	6.4	6.9	5.6
GDP per capita	3.1	3.3	2.0
Agriculture, livestock, forestry and fisheries	4.6	2.3	2.0
Mining	1.9	3.3	3.6
Petroleum and Petrochemicals	9.3	9.6	7.5
Manufacturing	7.1	8.6	5.9
Construction	7.2	9.7	8.3
Electricity	12.7	14.1	8.6
Trade	6.6	7.0	5.2
Transport and Communications	5.4	7.8	9.9
Government	6.6	7.6	10.5
Other Sources a/	5.4	5.4	3.7

Source: Weintraub, Sidney (1981), p. 273, Table 8-1. "Growth of Mexican Gross Domestic Product and Its Components, 1950-78."

a. Contains adjustment for banking services.

The pressures that emerged as a result of the ISI policies (increase in urban unemployment, and increase in inequalities in the distribution of wealth and income) were partially responsible for the student riots of Tlatelolco Plaza in Mexico City in 1968. This was a watershed in the economic history of Mexico, since it was the first sign of acute social and political discontent that had surfaced against the "Partido Revolucionario Institucional" (PRI), which had been in power for the last sixty years. It marked the first major defeat of the government in a country where the PRI had an absolute majority of both the lower house and the Senate of the national legislature. A country that had, until this time, enjoyed greater political stability than any of its neighbors in Latin America. The riots were thought by some to be a result of the structural imbalances that had emerged as a result of the import-substitution policies that had been followed [Kraft (1984), p. 31], specifically, the emergence of a dualistic economy that consisted of highly developed cities and underdeveloped rural areas. Typical consequences of dualistic development were observed--rural-urban migration (especially to Mexico City, Guadalajara, and Monterrey), rapid population growth in urban slums and capital-intensive growth, which not only increased unemployment, but also led to inequality in income and wealth distribution. Saul Trejo Reyes has estimated that in the early 1970s, 40 percent of the labor force was unemployed or underemployed.[8] Adalberto Garcia estimated that in 1968 Mexico's Gini coefficient (which was equal to 0.53 at the time) was higher than that of all the Latin American countries, excluding Brazil and Peru.[9] Public revenues were inadequate to support a policy of widespread public education, health, and other services. This prompted the Government to find ways to rectify this situation.

Two opposing views were prevailing at that juncture regarding the future path to be adopted by the incumbent president--Luis Echeverria Alvarez. The *structuralist view* (whose main proponents were Carlos Tello and Jose Andres Oteyza) was that the only way out of the situation would be to increase government expenditure, and direct its resources towards employment generation programs outside the three major cities' social and education programs, increased subsidization of the agricultural sector, and increased taxation of the private sector. The classical view (whose main proponent was Ortiz Mena--the chief of the Hacienda in 1968) was that an increase in government expenditures would overheat the economy and cause inflation, which would be translated into higher prices of Mexican exports, thereby causing a deterioration in the balance of payments. The fixed exchange rate regime, which was being pursued at the time, had resulted in an overvaluation of the peso, which, in turn, induced capital flight. Given the proximity of Mexico to the United States, it was believed that exchange controls would be ineffective in curtailing the outflow of capital from Mexico. The classical economists suggested the removal of protective tariffs and a reduction of subsidies so as to allow the forces of the free market to determine an equilibrium situation.

It was at this juncture that President Luis Echeverria Alvarez took office in December 1970. His primary task was to decide what path the Mexican economy would take, so as to deal effectively with the structural imbalances that prevailed at the time and resume growth. The issue of inequality in the distribution of wealth and income *had to* be addressed by the incumbent President.

MEXICO UNDER SHARED DEVELOPMENT, 1971-76

Under the previous regime of "Stabilizing Development," the policy had been to bring about growth by providing adequate incentives to the private sector, especially the manufacturing sector of Mexico. Although stable growth was, indeed, observed, this development strategy was accompanied by distortions and aggravated inequalities (especially between the rural and urban population). The usual side effects of a prolonged ISI policy were being observed by the time President Echeverria took office. (Table 2.5 and 2.6). The share of agriculture in GDP had fallen from about 20 percent in 1940 to around 10 percent by the later 1960s.[10] Urban areas showed large disparities in income, and disguised unemployment was on the rise. The pressure of migrants from the rural areas could not be borne by the major cities (Mexico City, Guadalajara, and Monterrey). Gerado Bueno (1971) and R. Looney (1985), among others, have contended that the economy began to slow down after 1965 because of the steep decline in agricultural output and the dwindling number of opportunities of efficient and viable import-substitution in Mexico.[11] In addition, the rapid industrialization that took place in the 1960s imposed a burden on the fiscal budget both from the revenue side and the expenditure side. The tax rate had a narrow base and was unable to support the growing expenditures (mainly because of the subsidies being provided to the private manufacturing enterprises). Mexican Development Banks (e.g., NAFINSA) were providing credit at highly subsidized rates. This easy credit policy had a detrimental effect on the effectiveness of monetary policy. Inflation began to show signs of appearing in the economy during the late 1960s.

Table 2.5
Components of Aggregate Demand, 1950-75 (percent of gross domestic product)

Year	CONSUMPTION			GROSS FIXED INVESTMENT			Exports[2]	Imports[2]
	Public	Private[1]	Total	Public	Private	Total		
1950	4.1	82.0	86.1	6.4	6.4	12.7	16.4	15.0
1951	4.2	83.0	87.3	5.5	9.8	15.3	14.6	17.3
1952	4.2	80.8	85.0	5.8	10.4	16.2	14.2	15.2
1953	4.3	83.1	87.4	5.3	8.9	14.2	13.4	15.0
1954	4.3	81.2	85.5	6.0	9.2	15.2	16.1	16.6
1955	4.3	79.7	84.0	5.3	10.1	15.4	17.1	16.6
1956	4.3	79.4	83.7	4.8	12.7	17.5	16.7	17.8
1957	4.5	81.0	85.5	5.1	12.1	17.3	13.7	16.6
1958	4.7	81.3	86.0	5.2	11.2	16.4	12.7	15.2
1959	4.6	80.8	85.4	5.1	10.7	15.9	12.3	13.5
1960	5.3	80.3	85.6	6.0	11.0	16.9	11.4	13.9
1961	5.3	81.0	86.3	6.8	9.0	15.8	11.3	12.8
1962	5.5	80.1	85.5	6.6	8.8	15.4	11.3	12.1
1963	5.7	78.8	84.5	7.6	9.1	16.6	10.9	12.0
1964	5.4	79.0	84.4	7.9	9.5	17.4	10.0	11.9
1965	7.0	77.0	84.0	5.6	11.9	17.5	9.9	11.4

Table 2.5 (continued)
Components of Aggregate Demand, 1950-75 (percent of gross domestic product)

Year	CONSUMPTION		GROSS FIXED INVESTMENT				Exports[2]	Imports[2]
	Public	Private[1]	Total	Public	Private	Total		
1950	4.1	82.0	86.1	6.4	6.4	12.7	16.4	15.0
1966	7.3	76.0	83.3	6.2	11.8	18.0	9.7	11.1
1967	7.3	75.2	82.6	7.4	12.0	19.5	9.0	11.1
1968	7.6	75.3	83.0	7.5	11.9	19.4	9.2	11.6
1969	7.7	74.5	82.2	7.6	11.8	19.4	9.9	11.5
1970	7.8	75.4	83.2	7.5	12.2	19.6	8.8	11.6
1971	8.1	76.1	84.2	5.6	12.2	17.8	8.8	10.8
1972	8.4	72.9	81.3	7.7	12.9	20.6	9.3	11.1
1973	8.9	71.7	80.6	8.8	12.9	21.8	9.7	12.1
1974	9.3	73.5	82.8	8.9	12.2	21.1	9.7	13.7
1975	9.9	73.1	83.0	9.8	12.0	21.8	8.0	12.7

Source: Computed by author using data from Nacional Financiera (1977).
1. Private Consumption includes changes in inventories.
2. Exports and Imports are of goods and services.

Table 2.6
Growth and Inflation in Mexico, 1965-83

Year	Real GDP	Consumer Prices	Wholesale Prices	Real Terms of: Wage Index	Real Terms of: Trade Index
	(Rates of Growth %)				
1965	6.5	n.a.	0.0	90.0	84.1
1966	6.9	n.a.	2.7	91.7	85.2
1967	6.3	n.a.	1.9	95.2	83.9
1968	8.1	n.a.	2.2	97.1	89.0
1969	6.3	4.3	4.0	100.7	88.0
1970	6.9	4.8	5.2	100.0	96.7
1971	4.2	5.2	3.0	100.5	100.0
1972	8.5	5.5	5.1	106.4	103.3
1973	8.4	21.3	25.3	103.5	115.2
1974	6.1	20.7	13.4	106.1	100.1
1975	5.6	11.2	13.5	110.7	97.8
1976	4.2	27.2	45.7	122.7	113.0
1977	3.4	20.7	18.1	125.1	113.0
1978	8.2	16.2	15.8	121.8	104.1
1979	9.2	20.0	19.9	119.9	113.1
1980	8.3	29.8	26.4	114.7	127.6
1981	7.9	28.7	27.2	125.6	124.3
1982	(0.1)	98.8	92.6	124.0	108.2
1983	(5.3)	80.8	88.0	84.2	98.8

Source: Gil-Diaz and Tercero (1988), pp. 365-66.
NOTES: 1. Rates of growth are for December-December.
2. Real wages for the manufacturing sector only. (1970 = 100)
3. For the Terms of Trade Index: 1971 = 100.

Chart 2.3
Gross Fixed Investment, 1950-75

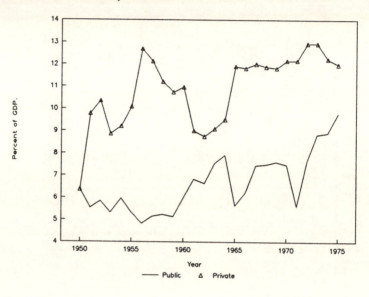

Chart 2.4
Mexico's Exports and Imports, 1950-75

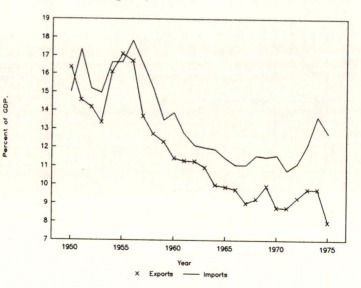

Chart 2.5
The Public Sector, Financing the Overall Deficit, 1965-83

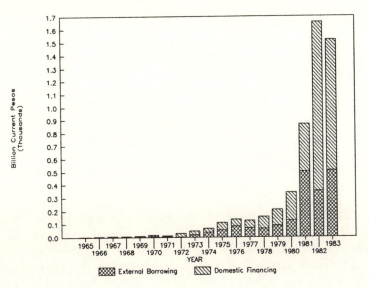

Chart 2.6
Exchange Rate Movements, 1965-89

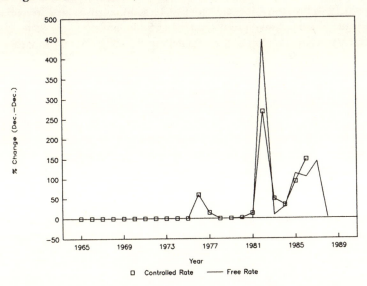

These structural imbalances were further aggravated by the rapid population growth that took place at the time resulting from the decline in the infant mortality rate and a rise in the birth rate. The industrialization process was giving rise to a growing urban labor force that emerged because of large rural-urban migration and population growth. It is important to note that disparities would result in the initial stages of any development strategy (not only ISI) in a country that started with inequalities in the first place. Those with assets would become richer in the early stages of growth (even in the case of an export-oriented growth strategy). The balance of payments problem and prolonged subsidization of the economy can, however, be attributed to ISI in Mexico.

In order to deal with the structural changes that had emerged as a result of the ISI policies of the previous regime, President Echevarria embarked on a strategy wherein the public sector was the "engine of growth." The Government, instead of providing more incentives to the private sector, began to increase spending on social infrastructure creation. Massive health, education, and public works projects were undertaken. At the same time, the Government did not reform the tax system in order to generate additional domestic resources to finance these large expenditures. So, on the one hand, the Government wanted to regain social stability and, on the other, it did not want to slow down the momentum that had been generated from the policies of the previous regime. Hence, budget deficits were created.

The Echeverria administration wanted to rectify the ills of the private private sector led growth by providing social services on a large scale, especially to the lower income groups. In addition, it wanted to maintain the value of the peso with respect to the U.S. dollar the United States being Mexico's major trading partner, accounting for a significant proportion of Mexico's exports and providing it with the majority of its receipts from tourism.

In 1971, Echeverria tried to follow restrictive policies and initiate tax reform, but failed on political and social grounds. Table 2.7 shows the behavior of the public sector finances and investment during 1965-83. The sharp increase in the role of the Government is quite apparent from these numbers. Although public sector revenues increased, they were not commensurate with the increase in public expenditures during this period. Even the Mexican banking system had to operate in such a way that it, in effect, accommodated the increase in government expenditure by providing "compulsory" loans to the Government. The Government also acquired funds through the legal reserve requirements of financial intermediaries in Mexico during the mid-1970s. This made monetary policy as an instrument

Table 2.7
Public Sector Finances, 1965-83 (as a % of GDP)

	1965	1966	1967	1968	1969	1970	1971	1972	1973	1974	1975	1976	1977	1978	1979	1980	1981	1982	1983
TOTAL REVENUE	17.9	17.1	17.3	17.5	17.8	17.5	17.0	17.3	18.7	19.6	21.6	22.1	22.7	22.6	23.1	25.2	23.9	26.3	30.5
o/w. Tax	6.5	7.0	7.1	7.6	7.7	7.3	7.3	7.3	8.0	8.2	9.5	9.8	10.1	11.1	10.7	10.9	10.6	9.9	10.2
TOTAL EXPENDITURE	18.6	18.2	19.4	19.4	19.7	20.7	19.0	21.2	23.9	25.2	29.8	29.9	27.7	27.8	28.3	31.8	36.9	41.9	38.5
o/w. Interest Pmts	0.8	0.8	1.2	1.0	1.1	1.8	1.5	1.7	1.7	1.8	2.1	3.1	2.9	3.0	3.2	3.5	5.0	8.2	12.4
Investment	3.7	3.5	5.0	5.1	5.3	6.5	4.8	6.3	6.2	6.0	7.7	7.8	6.6	8.7	9.5	8.9	12.7	9.7	7.7
o/w. PEMEX	0.4	0.4	0.8	0.5	0.4	0.4	0.7	0.6	0.8	0.8	1.1	1.5	1.8	2.5	2.8	2.8	3.8	2.9	1.9
ECONOMIC BALANCE	(0.7)	(1.1)	(2.1)	(1.8)	(1.9)	(3.2)	(1.9)	(3.9)	(5.2)	(5.6)	(8.2)	(7.7)	(5.0)	(5.2)	(5.1)	(6.6)	(13.0)	(15.6)	(8.0)
Fin. Intermediation	(0.1)	(0.1)	(0.2)	(0.3)	(0.3)	(0.3)	(0.3)	(0.6)	(1.2)	(1.2)	(1.1)	(1.5)	(1.3)	(1.1)	(1.3)	(1.0)	(1.1)	(1.3)	(0.5)
OVERALL BALANCE	(0.9)	(1.2)	(2.3)	(2.1)	(2.2)	(3.5)	(2.3)	(4.6)	(6.4)	(6.7)	(9.3)	(9.2)	(6.3)	(6.3)	(6.4)	(7.6)	(14.1)	(16.9)	(8.5)
PRIMARY BALANCE	0.0	(0.3)	(0.9)	(0.8)	(0.7)	(1.4)	(0.4)	(2.2)	(3.5)	(3.7)	(6.1)	(4.6)	(2.2)	(2.2)	(1.9)	(3.1)	(8.0)	(7.4)	4.4
Inflation Adjusted Overall Balance:	(1.0)	(1.3)	(2.4)	(2.2)	(1.9)	(3.6)	(2.2)	(4.7)	(5.8)	(6.2)	(9.4)	(8.5)	(5.2)	(5.3)	(5.2)	(5.6)	(11.7)	(11.9)	(5.4)
Financing the Overall Budget:	(0.9)	(1.2)	(2.3)	(2.1)	(2.2)	(3.5)	(2.3)	(4.6)	(6.4)	(6.7)	(9.3)	(9.2)	(6.3)	(6.3)	(6.4)	(7.6)	(14.1)	(16.9)	(8.5)
External Borrowing	0.3	1.0	2.0	1.3	1.5	1.1	1.0	0.3	2.7	3.8	4.6	5.7	3.4	2.5	2.7	2.8	8.2	3.6	2.9
Domestic Financing	0.6	0.3	0.3	0.9	0.7	2.4	1.3	4.2	3.6	3.0	4.7	3.6	2.9	3.7	3.7	4.8	5.9	13.3	5.7

Source: Gil-Diaz (1988), Banco de Mexico "Informe Anual" 1986, and World Bank.

of macroeconomic stabilization ineffective. In addition, as shown Table 2.8, the share of total domestic credit going to the private sector declined during the period. By the mid-1970s, inflationary pressures were growing in the economy. Sidney Weintraub (1981) has stated in this context:

> The decline in private sector confidence was reflected in capital flight estimated at $4 billion in the eighteen months preceding the devaluation. From December 1975 to December 1976, the increase in peso liabilities of the banking system was only 10 percent (less than half the percentage increase in the previous twelve months), whereas liabilities denominated in foreign currencies increased by 72 percent (more than double the percentage increase of the previous twelve months). [Weintraub (1981), p. 279]

In 1976, the Mexican economy had become increasingly "dollarized" and reflected the perceptions of the Mexican public that the economy was heading towards a serious crisis. In addition, by maintaining a fixed nominal exchange rate vis a vis the dollar, the peso was becoming overvalued in the face of the rising inflation and declining terms of trade.

Mexico had, indeed, maintained a stable currency (in real terms) earlier in the 1950s in an environment of domestic price stability, when its earnings from tourism, border transactions, and remittances from Mexican migrants in the United States were able to compensate for the Government's expenditures. However, in the mid-1970s, under an inflationary environment, the overvalued exchange rate encouraged massive imports of capital goods because they were relatively cheaper in peso terms, and this, in turn, distorted domestic factor prices. This distortion was further aggravated when import duties were relaxed as a matter of government policy. The overvalued exchange rate resulted in the firms in Mexico neglecting to produce for the international markets. Over time, this made Mexican industry less competitive in the international goods markets.

The overvalued exchange rate resulted in a large balance of payment deficits that were financed by borrowing from abroad. The total external debt of Mexico increased from $6.3 billion in 1971 to a staggering $27.3 billion by year end 1976. Almost all these debts were incurred by the Mexican public sector from commercial banks.

If we look at what President Echeverria had inherited when he came to office along with what he did to rectify the situation by the end of his term in year end 1976 we are left with the following dismal conclusions: compared to the previous *sexenio*, (i) the distribution of income in Mexico

Table 2.8
Total Domestic Credit in Mexico, 1970-76 (as a % of GDP, year-end)

Year	Domestic Credit	TO Public Sector	TO Private Sector
1970	44	22	22
1971	47	24	23
1973	47	25	22
1975	46	27	19
1976	42	27	15

Source: Weintraub (1981), p. 279.

has further deteriorated by 1976; Mexican agriculture was still neglected (only one project--Investment Program for Rural Development--was initiated in 1973); ISI was still the main development strategy being followed by the Government (except now it was driven by the public sector); the unemployment situation worsened and problem of inflation and capital flight had emerged.

Finally, in 1976, the economy collapsed because of extreme balance of payments pressures. The Government (which was in its last few months in office) made a last-ditch effort to stabilize the situation. Import controls were reinstituted, and government expenditures (mainly of parastatal enterprises) were cut. However, expenditure of other branches of the Government were maintained and so was the steady expansion in money supply. The current account deficit had increased to $3.7 billion for 1976, and the Banco de Mexico was experiencing a rapid decline in its international reserves (this was further exacerbated by capital flight).

On August 31, 1976, the peso was devalued by about 100 percent. This further eroded the public's confidence in the ability of the Government to rectify the situation, and in anticipation of the stabilization policies the next Government would inevitably have to take, large capital outflows took place and there were severe threats of runs on banks in Mexico. The situation had gotten out of hand when the next administration came into office at the end of that year.

Manuel Gollas summarized the inherent problem in the Mexican economy at the time by stating:

> Ironically, in the advanced stages of our import substitution period we ended up importing more since large quantities of capital and intermediate goods were now imported in order to produce what we were substituting. Our import substitution policies generated more imports than it replaced. [Gollas (1987), p. 79]

MEXICO, 1976-82: THE DEBT CRISIS EMERGES

Immediately after the Lopez Portillo administration took office in December 1976, an IMF stabilization program was agreed upon whereby the usual policies of trade liberalization, a restrictive monetary policy, and fiscal retrenchment were implemented. In 1977, the policies did, in fact, have beneficial results. The fiscal deficit was reduced from 9.9 percent of GDP in year end 1976 to 6.7 percent of GDP in year end 1977, the inflation rate declined from 27.2 percent per annum to 20.7 percent per annum, and the deficit in the current account was reduced. However, GDP growth had declined and unemployment increased (which was aggravated by the high population growth rate).[12] Total investment continued to decline.

After the first year of the stabilization program under the auspices of the IMF, large oil reserves were discovered in Mexico. Proven reserves increased from 6.4 billion barrels at year end 1975 to 16 billion by late 1977.[13] The Mexican government prepaid the IMF and suspended the three-year adjustment program after the first year. In turn, a policy of extensive public sector expansion was adopted. What followed was four years of rapid growth, the "Mexican miracle," with GDP growing at more than 8 percent, on average, for the period 1978-81. In addition, total fixed investment rose from about 20 percent of GDP in 1977 to almost 26 percent by 1981. Unlike the Echeverria regime, *both* public and private investment grew during these four years. It was believed at the time that the discovery of oil had strengthened Mexico's economic base and that it could support the increased role of the public sector in the economy. In the meantime, the Government postponed the much-needed reforms at the end of the Echeverria regime, which still continued to exist.

Investment was accelerated by the national petroleum company, PEMEX, in oil exploration and construction of pipelines, refineries, and petrochemicals. Proven reserves continued to increase. Oil exports increased from 200,000 barrels a day in 1977 to more than a million barrels a day by 1981. This was taking place at a time when the international oil price had more than doubled (between 1975-80). However, export earnings did not grow as fast as the growing public sector deficit. Most of this was financed by external borrowing. The Mexican private sector and commercial banks (e.g., Banamex, Bancomer, among others) increased as well between 1978-81. By 1982, PEMEX itself had borrowed $20 billion, which was equivalent to 20 percent of GDP, from abroad. Direct foreign investment in Mexico also increased during this period.

Mexico's external debt owed to commercial bank creditors abroad increased from $33 billion in 1979 to $72 billion in 1982 (which accounted for over 3/4 of Mexico's total external debt in1982).[14] After Mexico struck oil, its credit worthiness in the international financial markets improved significantly, even though just over a year ago Mexico was considered a bad credit risk to its commercial bank creditors.

The oil price in the international markets was $34 per barrel and was expected to remain at this level, if not increase, during the next few years. Mexico's ruling party in the Government (PRI) had enjoyed sixty years of stable, absolute majority and the banks considered Mexico's Government to be in complete control of economic activity and the trade unions and the military. This political position was unchallenged during this period. The commercial banks abroad also were "overliquid" because of deposits of petrodollars that they were acquiring as a result of the increase in oil prices. With the economic recession in the industrialized nations at the time, Mexico was perceived to be ripe with opportunities for receiving loans from banks. Zedillo (1985) stated in this context:

> Fierce competition among foreigners to grant new loans to the Mexican Government and to public enterprises was common during the booming years. In a matter of hours and days, important credit lines could be arranged. Putting together Eurocredit syndications was not a difficult task at all; there was always an excess demand to subscribe them. [Zedillo (1985), pp. 259-261]

For example, when Bank of America was arranging a publicly guaranteed loan of $1 billion in 1979, the international banking community provided $2.5 billion.[15] Ingenious ways were devised to go around the limits to lending by U.S. banks to a single entity specified in the U.S. banking regulations (e.g., by setting up distinct public sector entities in the same industry and then establishing automatic lines of credit with numerous U.S. and foreign banks).

Although Mexico was easily able to acquire funds from abroad, the way they were being utilized in the economy exacerbated the disparities and disequilibrium situation that existed at the time Lopez Portillo took office. Gollas has commented on this development by stating that: "By making it easy to earn foreign exchange, oil distracted our attention from the urgent need to promote (non-oil) exports." [Gollas (1985), p. 81]

As mentioned earlier, the revenues from increased oil exports during 1978-82 were not enough to compensate for the growing public expenditure. Expansionary monetary policy and foreign borrowing had to fill the financing gap.

The outcome of this massive increase in government expenditures would not have been so critical if the resources had been used efficiently and in productive investment projects. It is now common knowledge in the profession that a large share of foreign borrowing returned abroad as capital flight. Estimates of this magnitude of this capital outflow from Mexico are varied. Table 2.9 summarizes the different estimates of capital flight that have been put forth in the profession. These estimates do not account for

Table 2.9
Capital Flight in Mexico, 1977-85 (U.S.$ billion)

Year	Cumby & Levich	ALTERNATIVE ESTIMATES Zedillo	Buffie
1977	5.0	0.7	1.0
1978	1.8	0.1	0.6
1979	2.4	0.2	1.1
1980	6.8	(0.7)	3.9
1981	8.6	9.7	14.0
1982	7.2	8.2	9.0
1983	11.7	2.4	3.4
1984	6.0	2.3	3.7
1985	--	1.9	3.8
Total			
1977-82:	31.7	18.3	29.6
1977-85:	--	24.9	40.4

Source: Buffie (1989), Table 7.5, p. 152.

the capital flight that might have occurred via underinvoicing of imports and overinvoicing of exports.[16]

From 1980 onwards, the economy was showing signs of having the "Dutch Disease" or as Menacham Katz (1989) calls it, "The Petroleum Syndrome." Gulati (1984) has defined the "Dutch Disease" as a situation where an increase in a nation's natural resource endowment is followed by the *disease* of nominal wage increases and an appreciation of the real exchange rate.[17] Specifically, the increase in international oil prices (along with the discovery of large petroleum reserves in Mexico) led to a shift in the consumption possibilities frontier in the direction of increased availability of tradeables. This would result in a "resource movement affect" (à la Cordon) away from the nontradeable sector and non-oil-related industries. This implies a reduction in the output of nontradeable goods relative to the tradeable goods output (especially, in oil-related industries). The price of non-tradeables tends to rise, as a result of which inflationary pressures emerge in the domestic economy. When, in addition to this, the nominal exchange rate is fixed (or is adjusted at a slower rate than is appropriate for purchasing power parity), the real exchange rate appreciates. This artificially lowers the price of imported goods relative to nontradeable goods.

The behavior of the real exchange rate, in the long run, depends on the relative factor intensities of the tradeable and nontradeable goods. In the case of Mexico, the oil-related sector is relatively capital intensive and so were the sectors the Government was promoting (because of its public-sector-led ISI strategy). This resulted in the decline in agricultural output and massive rural-urban migration. Given the social and political implications of the declining real wages and the increased urban unemployment that followed, the Government had to increase expenditures on the provision of subsidized urban social services and urban infrastructure projects.

The increasing revenues of the oil sector (especially PEMEX) induced labor unions to demand higher real wages on the grounds that they also wanted to share in the windfall gains of Mexico's oil boom. The Government believed it politically expedient to grant such wage increases but since PEMEX was a parastatal entity, the wages of other parastatal workers also had to be increased. Sweder Van Wijnbergen (1982) has developed a model where nominal wages are indexed to the Consumer Price Index (CPI) (proxy for inflation in the economy). As the real exchange rate appreciates, the real wages are increased in terms the prices of traded goods but decline in terms of the prices of nontradeables. He has shown that whether unemployment results or not depends on (a) the share of tradeable to nontradeable goods in the CPI, and (b) the elasticity of demand in each sector relative to the wage rate in that sector. This, in turn, depends on the elasticity of substitution in production and the labor intensity in each sector.

The distortion in the labor market, together with the policy of absorbing the unemployed into unproductive public sector jobs (i.e., increase in disguised unemployment) in Mexico that occurred during the early 1980s actually resulted in the *fall* in real output of the non-oil sectors of the economy.

Zedillo (1985) has stated in this context that: "External disequilibrium was just the tip of the iceberg. The most notable evidence of disarray in the Mexican economy was the unchecked expansion in aggregate demand, led by the growth in public expenditure." [Zedillo (1985), p. 272]

Not only was expenditure by PEMEX increased between 1978-81, but other public enterprises as well as private consumption and investment followed suit. The pressures and bottlenecks caused by this increase in aggregate demand were accompanied by an expansionary monetary policy. The inflation rate, which had been brought under control in 1976-77 (during the IMF adjustment program), increased once again to about 30 percent by 1980. In the meantime, the nominal exchange rate was kept fixed relative to the U.S. dollar. This led to the real appreciation of the peso in the face of the rapidly growing inflation.

The growing stock of external debt meant larger interest payments each year. This was translated into a larger current account deficit. Nevertheless, the Government miscalculated the behavior of oil prices and international interest rates in the momentum of the oil boom and its overheated economy.

In this context, Zedillo has stated:

The 1981 budget overlooked not only internal bottlenecks but also conditions abroad. Perhaps the most dramatic example of this miscalculation is provided by the projections on the value of crude exports for 1981. The budget assumed that Mexico could export a volume 75 percent higher at a price of 10 percent higher than in 1980, although prices were already above $30 a barrel and the world economy had started to enter a deep recession. [Zedillo (1985) p. 273]

From June 1981, the results of the miscalculations of the Government became an unfortunate reality. The price of oil in the international markets plunged, and interest rates abroad increased. The economic recession in the United States (Mexico's most important trading partner) implied a decline in the demand for Mexican exports. Increased debt service payments and lower export earnings meant larger current account balance of payments deficits. These were financed by borrowing from abroad. The stock of debt outstanding and disbursed from foreign creditors had reached $86 billion in year end 1982, of which about $60 billion were public and publicly guaranteed medium-and long-term debt (MLT); $26 billion in short-term debt were owed to foreign creditors. Of the total MLT debt of Mexico in 1982, $47 billion were owed to commercial banks. Most of Mexico's short-term debt was also borrowed from commercial banks abroad [World Bank, "World Debt Tables," 1989-90]

When the international oil prices began to decline in mid-1981, instead of lowering its price, PEMEX tried to follow a marketing strategy, wherein they announced that they perceived this decline in oil prices to be temporary and asked importers abroad to continue to pay a higher price per barrel of oil than was available in the international petroleum market or else they would be taken off a list of "preferred" customers. When the price would go back up again, PEMEX would only sell to those importers on this list. This strategy worked for only a few weeks; thereafter, importers refused to pay the high price. In 1981, Mexico exported $14 billion worth of oil instead of the $20 billion that was in their projections.

In order to reduce the balance of payments deficit, a devaluation of the peso was inevitable and quite correctly being anticipated by the Mexican private sector. The result was a massive amount of capital flight abroad. Foreign exchange reserves in the Banco de Mexico were quickly dwindling. In order to control inflation without reducing government expenditures, the Banco de Mexico followed a contractionary monetary policy and raised domestic interest rates. The real interest rate became higher than international interest rates. Therefore, Mexican firms also borrowed from abroad. Most of this borrowing was short-term in nature. The Government announced that they would make every effort to reduce public expenditures, but, in fact, no such action was taken. Mexico's total external debt increased by $23 billion in 1981 alone, and this was primarily borrowed by the Mexican public sector. The external borrowing by the Mexican commercial banks was also relent to the public sector.

By 1982, confidence in the Mexican economy on the part of foreign observers was on the decline, and the public and private sector began having increasing difficulties in acquiring credit. Within the country, the Mexican public was losing confidence in the Government's ability and motivation to rectify the situation (given that this was the last year of the Lopez Portillo administration). This was gleaned from the increasing capital outflows. In addition, in anticipation of a major devaluation of the peso, others were increasingly directing their savings to U.S. dollar-denominated accounts, which existed at the time in the Mexican banking system ("Mexdollar" accounts).

On February 17, 1982, the peso was devalued by 40 percent, and the Government announced a stabilization program to deal with the growing public sector deposit. This included a 3 percent reduction in the federal budget, reduction in tariffs on as many as 1,500 goods (especially capital goods and raw materials), the tightening of price controls, and an emergency wage increase of a maximum of 10 percent. However, a few weeks after the devaluation of the peso, the Government announced another 30 percent increase in the minimum wage. The Government announced that it would increase prices of goods and services produced by the public sector, but nothing significant was implemented.[18] In effect, the adjustment program that was announced by the Government was ineffective in rectifying the growing distortions and external debt in Mexico.

In order not to devalue the peso further, the Government used up its international reserves and access to any new loans it could acquire from abroad. The rolling over of short-term credits, which had been granted by the banks in the past, was becoming increasingly difficult. Short-term credit, when available, was only at shorter maturities and higher spreads [Zedillo (1985)].

In August 1982, the Government announced a two-tier exchange system in order to deal with the capital flight problem. This, however, increased speculative transactions involving the peso. A week later, the Government announced that it would only pay back the deposits of the Mexicans in the "Mexdollar" accounts in domestic currency at an exchange rate of 69.3 pesos per U.S. dollar while the free market rate fluctuated between 100-150 pesos/$. Banks were also ordered to suspend all foreign exchange transactions until further notice.

In this context, Katz (1989) stated that:

These actions, however, were viewed by the public as a sign of inability to cope with the situation. Capital outflows accelerated and foreign exchange reserves were being depleted at 200-300 million dollars a day. By mid-August, the Mexican authorities were left with no foreign exchange reserves. Some $20 billion in short-term loans were due but the foreign banks refused to roll them over. [Katz (1989)]

It was at this time that the secretary of finance, Jesus Silva Herzog, met with the commercial banks and requested a three-month moratorium on principal repayments and the restructuring of Mexico's external debt obligations.

While the Mexican debt negotiators were abroad, President Lopez Portillo nationalized the Mexican banking system on September 1, 1982. Strict foreign exchange controls were imposed. Import licensing was also instituted and a price freeze announced. In addition, the Government lowered domestic interest rates, and deepened the subsidization of goods and services. The peso was devalued once again. These actions resulted in the complete loss of confidence on the part of both foreign creditors and the Mexican public. Capital flight accelerated, and inflation was recorded at *10 percent per month*.

It was under these precarious circumstances that the new Government under President Miguel de la Madrid took office on December 1982. The International Debt Crisis had emerged by then, since fourteen other countries had declared their inability to meet their debt service obligations to their external commercial bank creditors.

NOTES

1. See Bodayla (1982) for details on the debate over Mexican insolvency in the early twentieth century.

2. Source: Francisco Gil Diaz (1989), pp. 10 - 11.

3. See Francisco Gil Diaz (1989), and Jean Bazant (1968) for details on the Suarez-Lamont Agreement.

4. See Cardoso and Levy (1988), pp. 355 - 357 for details on nominal and effective rates of protection in Mexico during this period.

5. See Ernesto Zedillo (1981) "External Public Indebtedness in Mexico: Recent History and Future, oil bounded optimal growth." Ph.D. Dissertation, Yale University.

6. The real exchange rate being defined as the ratio of the Mexican wholesale price index and the weighted average index of prices of its main trading partners (in pesos).

7. Stabilizing development.

8. See Saul Trejo=Reyes, (1977) "La Politica Laboral," in Gerardo M. Bueno (ed.) *Opciones de Politica Economica en Mexico Despues de la Devaluacion* Mexico D.F.: Editorial Tecnos, p. 150.

9. See Adalberto R. Garcia, "La Distribucion del Ingreso en Mexico," *Demografia y Economia*, Vol. 8, No. 2 (1974).

10. Source: Katz (1989), p. 372.

11. Buffie (1989) has criticized all the above observations regarding the inadequacy of employment growth, the growing inequality of income, and the diminishing growth potential in Mexico at the time mainly on the grounds that the available data are unreliable and not comparable over time. By his reasoning, it would follow that the student riots of 1968 and the growing number of urban slums around the major cities at that time were mere historical aberrations or very difficult to explain.

12. Source: Buffie (1989), p.147.

13. Source: Zedillo (1985), p. 259.

14. Source: Katz (1989), p. 377.

15. Source: Kraft, pp. 19 - 20

16. See S. Gulati (1987), "A Note on Trade Misinvoicing," in Donald Lassard and John Williamson (eds.), *Capital Flight and Third World Debt*, Washington, D.C.: Institute for International Economics.

17. The real exchange rate being defined as the relative price of Mexico's nontradeables to its tradeables.

18. See Ariel Buira (1983) and Zedillo (1985) for details on developments just months before Mexico declared the 1982 moratorium.

3

Mexico in the Post-1982 Period:
Adjustment Without Growth

In the previous chapter, it was shown that between 1940-81 Mexico experienced rapid economic growth with GDP growing at about 6 percent per annum, on average. This was possible because of the development strategy that was being pursued at that time--one of import-substitution industrialization (ISI). The size of the public sector was expanded, and incentives were given to the private sector as well as foreign investors to flourish.

However, this ISI process put a burden on the Government's budget on both the revenue and expenditure sides. Structural imbalances had also developed from the systematic neglect of the agricultural sector, which intensified inequalities. Social and economic discontent that was prevailing at the time was dealt with by increased spending by the Government on health, education, public works, and subsidies without increasing the tax base. This caused a further pressure on the Government's budget. The Government chose to finance this deficit through external borrowing, which was freely available at that time, and even more so, once large oil reserves were discovered in Mexico (1976-77).

The increase in revenues from oil exports in the early 1980s was not enough to cover the growing government expenditure, and it was becoming apparent that the Mexican economy was beginning to suffer from a "petroleum syndrome" (a la Menachem Katz [1989]).[1] Non-oil exports remained stagnant. The dramatic increase in aggregate demand and inadequate supply response created inflationary pressures on the economy that were fueled by an accommodating monetary policy. As inflation accelerated, the nominal exchange rate was maintained at a fixed level relative to the U.S. dollar, which, in turn, led to an appreciation of the peso in real terms by some 30 percent during 1978-82.

The growing imbalances continued on to the year 1982, which was the last year of the Lopez Portillo administration, and the loss of confidence on the part of the public resulted in severe capital flight. In addition, as international interest rates rose in the early 1980s, the burden of debt service payments was becoming unmanageable, as the public sector budget increased, and the peso became increasingly overvalued. The Mexican public, which had lost confidence in the ability of the Government (which was in the last few months of its term), came to expect that the next government would ultimately tax their assets in order to service the growing debt. Private investors did not want to invest because of similar fears. Therefore, as long as the Government was able to acquire foreign loans readily, the Mexican public chose to shift their assets abroad (i.e., capital flight). Estimates of this massive acquisition of foreign assets have been provided in the previous chapter.

By August 1982, the Government had no international reserves in its coffers to service its external debt and, therefore, declared a moratorium on principal payments to all creditors and on interest payments to private creditors. During the next few months, fourteen other countries followed suit. Mexico had brought the International Debt Crisis to the forefront.

In this chapter, the developments after Mexico's declaration of a moratorium on debt service payments to foreign creditors are examined. Three aspects will be highlighted in the discussion: (1) the domestic policies and adjustment effort on the part of the Mexican government, which were instituted in order to rejuvenate public confidence and give private individuals the incentive to bring about the return of flight capital, increase domestic investment, and stimulate economic growth; (2) the role and trends in direct foreign investment (including a discussion of the domestic efforts of the Mexican Government to bring about increased investment from abroad); and (3) developments in Mexico's debt renegotiation process. The question that will be addressed in this context is to what extent did the adjustment process and developments on the debt front change the structure of economic incentives in order to improve the general efficiency of the economic system, and bring about growth and stability?

GETTING THE HOUSE IN ORDER

In the last few months of 1982, after Mexico had declared a moratorium on debt service payments to its private external creditors, emergency loans were put into place under the auspices of the U.S. government (who provided $1.4 billion) and the Bank for International

Settlements (BIS), while a debt restructuring package was being negotiated with Mexico's commercial bank creditors.

On December 1, 1982, President Miguel de la Madrid took office and embarked on an economic adjustment program--"Programa Imediato de Reordinacion Economica" or *National Development*--that was geared towards dealing with overcoming the crisis, and returning the economy to a path of stable and sustained economic growth. This was to be achieved by following a two-pronged approach: (1) immediate short-term economic adjustment; and (2) long-term structural change. Specifically, the public sector deficit was to be reduced through a tight budgetary policy, and a thorough revision of subsidies, and the tax system, and the pattern of public expenditure. The current account deficit would be reduced--mainly through an appropriate exchange rate policy and a comprehensive program to promote non-oil exports. This was expected to bring about an increase in domestic saving so as to reduce Mexico's reliance on foreign financing. The Government stipulated that it would endeavor to enhance the efficiency of the economy through a revision of the foreign trade practices that prevailed at the time. A restructuring of state enterprises and their modernization were also proposed.[2] Table 3.1 follows pattern of GDP growth and inflation in the economy during the last for presidential *sexenios*.

The policy of fiscal discipline was inevitable, given the cut off of external financing after the declaration of the moratorium in 1982. After having been able to maintain noninterest current account (NICA) deficits for three decades, Mexico had to generate surpluses in the NICA for the next few years in order to bring about sustained growth. Real GDP growth rates had been higher than the real interest rate on external debt prior to 1982. However, the gap between real interest rates on external debt and real GDP growth went from minus 6.3 percent in 1980-81 to plus 10.5 percent in 1983. Differences this high meant that even without deficits in the NICA the burden of debt would increase rapidly, simply through the compounding effect of interest on debt inherited from the past [van Wijnbergen (1989), p.2].

The adjustment program that was implemented between 1983-85 did, indeed, bring some of the favorable results that were desired--there was an improvement in public finances. The overall public sector deficit (in nominal terms) declined from 17.1 percent of GDP in 1982 to 8.4 percent in 1985. This was achieved by rigidly following restrictive public sector operating expenditure policies, a stringent public investment policy, and a reduction in subsidies. Prices of goods produced and sold in the public

Table 3.1
Growth and Inflation in Mexico in the Last Four Sexenios, 1965-87 (% per annum)

Period	President	Growth*	Inflation
1965-70	Diaz Ordaz	3.4	3.6
1971-76	Echeverria	2.7	14.1
1977-82	Lopez Portillo	3.1	30.5
1983-88	de la Madrid	(2.5)	90.0

* Growth rates provided for 1983-87.
Source: Dornbusch (1988), p. 238.

sector were increased, and tax rates increased. Interest rates on preferential credit granted by Mexican Development Banks and financial institutions were increased so as to make the rates comparable to the cost of funds. During the 1983-85 period, the volume of subsidized credit was decreased in real terms. These actions led to the reduction in the subsidization in the economy that existed prior to 1983. Trade liberalization measures were also successfully pursued. Measures were also taken to promote direct foreign investment in Mexico. Higher yields on domestic financial assets, resulting from increased interest rates, along with a gradual improvement in the level of confidence of the public in the Mexican economy, brought about an increase in financial savings.[3]   Table 3.2 shows the key macroeconomic indicators of Mexico between 1980 and 1998.

The stringent adjustment policies that were being pursued during 1983-85 did have some negative effects associated with them. Most importantly, there was a contraction in GDP, and a drastic reduction in private and public investment (which would have adverse long-term implications on growth). Although, output recovered in 1984 and 1985, the rate of growth of GDP remained well below its historical levels. The rate of growth of employment also did not keep pace with the rate of growth of the labor force during 1984 and 1985 as well. Real wages also declined between 1983-85 as a result of which there was a real devaluation of the peso. This real depreciation of the peso implied that Mexico had to incur capital losses on its external debt.

The severe compression of imports that took place during 1983-85 was detrimental to Mexico's industrial production. Most of Mexico's imports at that time were intermediate goods and capital equipment. The contraction in imports that resulted because of import controls and the real devaluation of the peso led to a deceleration in economic activity. This, in turn, reduced the demand for labor and discouraged investment by reducing the productivity of capital equipment.[4] Restrictions on importing capital goods also implicitly increased the cost of capital goods. The terms of trade also became unfavorable for Mexico.

In criticism of the adjustment process followed by the Mexican Government in 1983-85, Jaime Ros (1987) has contended:

Although the conditions for their application were comparatively favorable, the fragility and internal contradictions of this policy approach progressively eroded the room for manoeuvre that had been obtained through a large short-term external adjustment. Consequently, after three years of depression and large relative price adjustments, the country was left in continuous economic and financial troubles with no

Table 3.2
Mexico: Macroeconomic Indicators, 1980-88

	1980	1981	1982	1983	1984	1985	1986	1987	1988
Real GDP Growth (%)	8.3	8.8	(0.6)	(4.2)	3.6	2.6	(3.8)	1.7	1.3
Growth in Real GDP per capital (%)	5.4	6.3	(2.9)	(6.3)	1.4	0.4	(5.9)	(0.3)	(0.6)
Population Growth (%)	2.8	2.4	2.3	2.3	2.2	2.2	2.1	2.0	1.9
Inflation Rate (%):									
Change in CPI, Dec-Dec	29.8	28.7	98.8	80.8	59.2	63.7	105.7	159.2	51.7
Change in PPI, Dec-Dec	-	27.6	93.5	80.2	60.1	61.1	102.3	166.5	37.3

Source: Banco de Mexico, "Indicadores Economicos," February 1990.

Chart 3.1
Real Domestic Interest Rates, Non-monetary Peso Denominated Debt

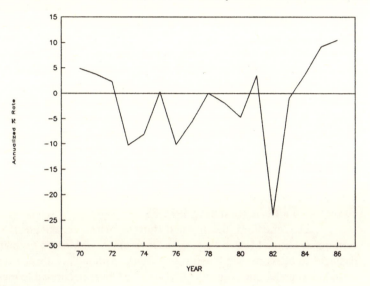

Chart 3.2
Nominal Interest Rates, 1978-89 (annual percentage rates)

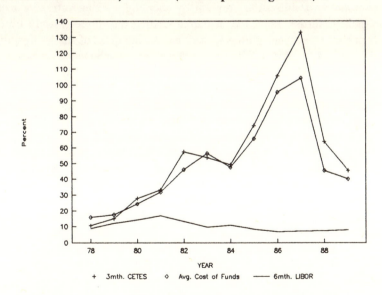

significant long-term structural adjustment having taken place. [Ros (1987), p. 68]

Although the short-run crisis situation of 1982 had been successfully tackled, the long-run structural adjustment could not be sustained beyond 1985. In addition to the effects of domestic contraction of economic activity and the aforementioned factors, the external environment deteriorated considerably from 1985. The drastic reduction in oil prices and increase in international interest rates resulted in a decrease in export income (thereby increasing the current account deficit) and an increase in the debt service burden. This was further aggravated by the continuing real depreciation of the peso at the time, since the economy had to produce and export more in order to generate enough foreign exchange earnings to meet its debt service obligations. In view of the deteriorating terms of trade, declining industrial production and stagnation in GDP, and the emergence of inflationary expectations, expectations of the private sector were adversely affected and capital outflows increased. Table 3.3 shows the behavior of Mexico's current account balance during 1980-88.

The situation deteriorated further when the September 1985 earthquake struck Mexico City. The Government of Mexico estimated total damages to be more than 2 percent of GDP. Although reconstruction costs were to be spread out over several years, the Government had to incur large expenses in the last quarter of 1985 and early 1986. This increased the pressure on public finances, imports, and domestic credit.

To counteract this situation, the Government further reinforced its economic stabilization program by adopting a more restrictive monetary policy, further reduction in public sector expenditure (mainly by cutting public investment further), and an acceleration of trade liberalization measures. An additional package of counteractive measures was implemented on July 24, 1986. These measures consisted of a 20 percent devaluation of the controlled exchange rate, a further, reduction in public sector expenditure, increase in domestic interest rates, and strengthening of the tax collection machinery in the Government.

Despite these measures, the economy continued to deteriorate. The real exchange rate began to appreciate, and inflation resumed its upward trend. The public sector deficit and balance of payments deteriorated. The economy was slipping into a recession, and all the gains of the previous three years were being neutralized. The economy had reached a stage of adjustment fatigue, and the policy makers believed that without growth, any further adjustment was politically and socially unacceptable.

On July 21, 1986, the *Programa de Aliento y Crecimiento* (PAC) was

Table 3.3
Composition of External Trade, 1980-88 (US$ Billions)

	1980	1981	1982	1983	1984	1985	1986	1986	1988
EXPORTS	15.5	20.1	21.2	22.3	24.2	21.7	16.0	20.7	20.7
o/w. Petroleum (%)	67.1	72.6	78.8	71.7	68.6%	68.2%	39.4%	41.6%	32.5%
Manufacturing (%)	19.4%	16.7%	14.2%	20.6%	23.1%	22.9%	44.4%	48.0%	56.3%
IMPORTS	18.9	23.9	14.4	8.6	11.3	13.2	11.4	12.2	18.9
o/w. capital (%)	27.4%	31.6%	31.3%	25.7%	23.1%	24.2%	25.9%	21.6%	21.4%
Trade Balance	(3.4)	(3.8)	6.8	13.8	12.9	8.5	4.6	8.5	1.8
NON-INT. Current a/c.	(2.6)	(3.9)	4.9	15.4	15.5	11.5	6.7	12.3	5.9
Interest Payments [1]	6.1	9.8	11.2	10.0	11.3	10.2	8.4	8.3	8.8
CURRENT a/c. BALANCE	(8.7)	(13.6)	(6.2)	5.4	4.2	1.2	(1.7)	4.0	(2.9)

Source: Computed by author using data from Banco de Mexico "Indicadores Economics", various issues and the World Bank.
Note: 1. Interest payments on total debt taken from World Bank, "World Debt Tables," 1989-90.

Chart 3.3
Public Sector Deficits, 1980-87

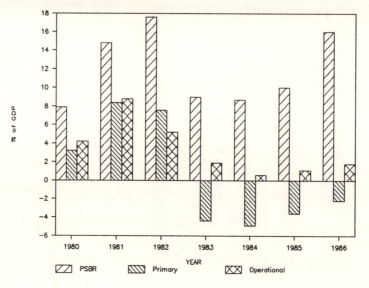

Chart 3.4
Investment in Mexico, 1950-87

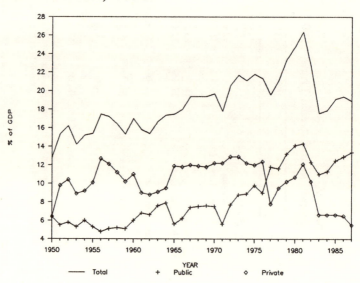

announced by the Government. The objective of the Government was stated to be "the attainment of sustained growth in a climate of financial stability."[5] Policy reforms were to be undertaken in order to eliminate structural rigidities. The Government wanted to bring about a major reorientation towards exploiting the benefits of international trade by vigorously promoting non-oil exports. The medium-term objectives of this strategy were stated to be the following:[6]

- To protect output and employment in order to bring about sustained economic growth.
- To reduce inflationary pressures that resulted from the oil shock.
- To prevent real wages from falling further.
- To manage public finances more efficiently so as to free resources for public investment.
- To promote private investment actively through proper incentives.
- To increase non-oil exports.
- To reduce the net transfer of resources abroad.

To enable their access to foreign financing in case of further deterioration as a result of external shocks, the Government proposed a strategy wherein foreign creditors would automatically provide financing in the event that the oil price fell below $9 per barrel in the international market and/or if the rate of growth of the Mexican economy, as projected in the plan, would not materialize by the first quarter of 1987. Details of Mexico's debt restructuring agreement will be discussed later on in this chapter. The additional resources were to be used to stimulate private investment, and would be directed to high-yielding projects that would have significant backward and forward linkages in the Mexican economy. The Government proposed to pursue exchange rate and interest rate policies that would maintain positive and internationally competitive yields in real terms. This was expected to increase domestic savings, improve confidence in the economy, and, in turn, bring about the return of flight capital and increase private investment, thereby leading to economic growth.

Van Wijnbergen (1989) has stated that the Government, in effect, followed a policy of *de facto* targeting of the real exchange rate during the 1986-87 period, along with frequent adjustments in wages and costs. This introduced an element of inherent instability in the economy and led to adverse expectations on the outlook of the economy. At the end of 1987, the stock market crash and the temporary opportunity for buybacks of private debt, which was permitted in the 1987 debt restructuring agreement

Table 3.4
The Mexican Public Sector, 1980-88 (As a Percentage of GDP)

	1980	1981	1982	1983	1984	1985	1986	1987	1988
REVENUES	26.9	26.7	28.9	32.9	32.2	31.2	30.3	30.6	29.8
o/w. Petroleum Sector	7.3	7.3	9.9	14.2	13.0	11.5	9.0	9.8	7.5
EXPENDITURES	33.5	39.7	44.5	41.0	39.3	39.2	44.8	45.0	39.0
o/w. Capital Exp.	9.6	12.9	10.2	7.5	6.7	6.0	6.0	6.5	4.4
ECONOMIC DEFICIT*	6.5	13.0	15.6	8.1	7.1	8.0	14.9	15.1	10.7
Finan. Intermediation	1.0	1.1	1.3	0.5	1.4	1.5	1.1	1.0	1.6
FINANCIAL DEFICIT	7.5	14.1	16.9	8.6	8.5	9.5	16.0	16.1	12.3

Source: Banco de Mexico, "Indicadores Economicos," February 1990.
Note: * Adjusted by Banco de Mexico for differences in sources of financing.

Table 3.5
Public Sector Deficit, 1965-87 Alternative Definitions (% of GDP)

	Financial (PSBR)	Primary	Operational
1965-69	1.8	-	1.3
1970-74	5.1	-	2.7
1975-79	8.1	2.5	4.4
1980	7.9	3.2	4.2
1981	14.8	8.4	8.8
1982	17.6	7.6	5.2
1983	9.0	(4.4)	1.9
1984	8.7	(4.9)	0.6
1985	10.0	(3.6)	1.1
1986	16.0	(2.2)	1.8
1987	15.8	(4.9)	(1.2)

Source: Dornbusch (1988), pp. 258, 279, Tables 12 and A1.

( )   Denotes a surplus.

<u>Notes:</u>   Financial deficit (public sector borrowing requirement): Difference between revenues and expenditures, net of amortizations.

Primary deficit: Financial deficit minus total interest payments on external and interal debt.

with external creditors, led to a run on the peso. The Banco de Mexico incurred reserve losses, and a 37 percent depreciation of the peso was implemented. This further fueled inflation, and the Mexican public expected further exchange rate depreciations. Capital flight began to show its presence yet again. Triple-digit inflation was observed during the end of 1987, partially in response to a large nominal devaluation of the peso. Once again, there was no real growth in the Mexican economy as a result of the low investment rate and restrictive demand management policies. Table 3.4 and 3.5 show the behavior of Mexico's public sector deficit as a percent of GDP over time.

On December 1, 1988, the current president, Carlos Salinas de Gortari, took office. This was the first time after sixty years that the ruling party-- the Institutional Revolutionary Party (PRI)--faced a strong opposition in the elections from other political parties in Mexico. The incumbent president was determined to maintain the leading role of PRI and endeavored to modernize Mexico during his "sexenio" in office. His speeches made it quite apparent that he wanted a smaller and more efficient government, and wanted to maintain the reform process that was initiated by his predecessor, President Miguel de la Madrid. The present administration will have to work under a more democratic environment and wants to continue with its heroic trade liberalization measures. In addition, it is now embarking on a widespread privatization effort, wherein the national telephone company are has recently been privatized. A large copper mine is also under consideration for privatization. Table 3.6 shows the behavior of gross fixed investment as a percentage of GDP in Mexico between 1950-87. To tackle the problem of inflation and declining investment levels in the face of deteriorating real wages and terms of trade, the new administration negotiated a historic agreement between business labor and Government-- *The Economic Solidarity Pact* (Pacto)--which calls for an accelerated structural reform process. This includes further restrictive monetary and fiscal policy, and a freeze in the minimum wage and prices of basic goods produced in both the public and private sectors. The fundamental ingredient of the Pacto is the freezing of the nominal exchange rate against the U.S. dollar. This freeze had been extended at three-month intervals through the end of 1988. The Pacto was then renewed, with a few modifications, under a new agreement between the three parties until July 1990 as the *Pact for Stabilization and Growth* (PECE).[7]

The modifications that have been incorporated in PECE include:

- A one-shot increase in tariffs and prices of key inputs.
- A two-stage adjustment upward of the minimum wage.
  A *daily* devaluation of the exchange rate by one peso per dollar.

Table 3.6
Investment in Mexico, 1950-87 (as a percent of GDP)

| | GROSS FIXED INVESTMENT | | |
YEAR	Public	Private	Total
1950	6.4	6.4	12.8
1951	5.5	9.8	15.3
1952	5.8	10.4	16.2
1953	5.3	8.9	14.2
1954	6.0	9.2	15.2
1955	5.3	10.1	15.4
1956	4.8	12.7	17.5
1957	5.1	12.1	17.2
1958	5.2	11.2	16.4
1959	5.1	10.2	15.3
1960	6.0	11.0	17.0
1961	6.8	9.0	15.8
1962	6.6	8.8	15.4
1963	7.6	9.1	16.7
1964	7.9	9.5	17.4
1965	5.6	11.9	17.5
1966	6.2	11.8	18.0
1967	7.4	12.0	19.4
1968	7.5	11.9	19.4
1969	7.6	11.8	19.4
1970	7.5	12.2	19.7
1971	5.6	12.2	17.8
1972	7.7	12.9	20.6
1973	8.8	12.9	21.7
1974	8.9	12.2	21.1
1975	9.8	12.0	21.8
1976	9.0	12.4	21.4
1977	11.8	7.8	19.6
1978	11.6	9.5	21.1
1979	13.2	10.2	23.4
1980	14.1	10.7	24.8
1981	14.3	12.1	26.4
1982	12.3	10.2	22.5
1983	11.0	6.6	17.6
1984	11.3	6.6	17.9
1985	12.5	6.6	19.1
1986	12.9	6.5	19.4
1987	13.4	5.5	18.9

Source: Banco de Mexico,"Indicadores Economicos", Feb. 1990
Nacional Financiera (1977) "Statistics on The Mexican
Economy".

Recently, the Government announced that it would adjust the public sector prices more frequently but by smaller amounts, in line with inflation targets. Even in the agricultural sector, a more flexible pricing policy has been adopted. In May 1989, the foreign investment code was made more transparent and regulations relaxed. Details of these changes are provided in the next section of this chapter.

The Government has replaced global subsidies for basic food items with cheaper goods and more targeted subsidies to the poor. In 1989, $400 million were earmarked for budgetary support for agriculture, infrastructure, and social programs in Mexico's ten poorest states.

The policies implemented under the Pacto and PECE have, indeed, been successful in reducing inflation from 159 percent in 1987 to 20 percent in 1989. However, the current account balance has deteriorated from a deficit of $3 billion in 1988 to $5 billion in 1989. This has been partly as a result of the drought that has led to a reduction in Mexico's agricultural exports. The real exchange rate has appreciated during the period over which the nominal exchange rate was frozen (at a level linked to the U.S. dollar). Domestic interest rates are still higher than historical levels, although they declined by 20 percentage points within days after the announcement of the most recent debt reduction package with Mexico's commercial bank creditors. Two billion dollars in flight capital are said to have returned to Mexico as a result of this debt reduction operation.[8]

Over the period 1982-89, Mexico has come a long way towards bringing about long-term structural changes in its economy while, at the same time, dealing with its short-run problems. However, the end of the road is still in sight. The rate of investment (public and private) is well below desired levels. This will have adverse long-term implications on growth. In addition, the appreciation of the real exchange rate and speculation on the part of the public concerning future devaluation of the peso loom large. This is illustrated by the high domestic interest rates that are needed to induce the public to keep their savings within the domestic financial system. The stringent policy of fiscal austerity on the part of the Government has resulted in the postponement of much-needed expenditure on the maintenance of the social infrastructure in Mexico (roads, bridges, highways, and so forth). This will need to be addressed if sustained growth has to be achieved in the near future.

The observed decline in the domestic real interest rate and the return of flight capital that occurred after the July 1989 debt reduction operation clearly suggest the need to evaluate the link between domestic investment and the debt overhang in the context of the Mexican economy.

Having examined the stringent adjustment measures and the mixed results that have emerged in Mexico, it is now appropriate to turn to Mexico's dealings with its foreign investors and creditors in order to alleviate its debt-servicing difficulties and bring about sustained growth.

DIRECT FOREIGN INVESTMENT[9]

In this section, the role and potential for direct foreign investment (DFI) in Mexico are examined. DFI is another source of foreign financing, in addition to foreign borrowing, that is available to a LDC. DFI, along with investment by domestic nationals (private and public investment), plays a significant role in bringing about growth and alleviating a country's debt-servicing problems in the long run. By providing adequate incentives, a government in an LDC can attract resources from abroad that are used for productive investment in the economy.

In the case of Mexico, DFI is expected to play a crucial role as a source of financing and as a component of the any projected expansion in private investment that the Government would like to encourage in Mexico as part of its current development strategy.

We begin by discussing the different roles foreign investment would have to play in Mexico and then provide the main factors that affect the flow of DFI into the country: Recent changes in the investment code and tax policies will be discussed in this context. A brief assessment of the expected behavior of DFI given current adjustment efforts of the Mexican government and the external environment will be provided. A discussion of the "maquiladora" (in-bond) sector of Mexico is provided in Appendix B, and the possibility of portfolio investment in Mexico (via the Mexican Stock Exchange) by foreigners is examined in Appendix C of this chapter.

The Roles of Direct Foreign Investment

Direct foreign investment is expected to play three main roles in any LDC:

- *Balance of payments support*-In Mexico, as in other HICs the inflow of foreign capital is expected to finance part of its debt service obligations. Foreign investment is presumably cheaper than new loans, and also provides Mexico with a better risk-sharing profile in obtaining foreign capital.
- *Linkage effect on domestic private investment*-Foreign investment is expected to increase total private investment by complementing

investment by Mexican residents, and thereby increasing the rate of capital formation and, in turn, the rate of growth in the economy. Foreign firms would invest in Mexico as long as the expected rate of return on capital there was higher than what they would attain elsewhere (including the developed countries).

- *Technology Transfer*-Foreign investment is expected to improve the quality and productivity of capital in the country through the superior technology that is embodied in the capital this DFI brings with it. This advanced technology is not only scientific and technical in nature, but also include new managerial techniques and knowledge of external markets.

Recent Trends in Direct Foreign Investment

During 1973-79, the average share of DFI in GDP was only 0.38 percent. This share increased during the oil boom to an average of 1.1 percent of GDP between 1980-82. Between January 1983 and December 1987, total investment from abroad reached $10 billion. This drastic increase accounts for 49 percent of the total stock of direct foreign investment that had accumulated as of year-end 1987 ($20.9 billion). Of this total, $2.9 billion came to Mexico via the debt-equity conversion program.[10]

During 1986 and 1987, DFI increased at a much faster rate than domestic private fixed capital formation. This increase was particularly marked in 1987, when the inflow of capital from abroad increased from $1.5 billion in 1986 to $3.2 billion in 1987. Table 3.7 provides a breakdown of the foreign investment inflows into Mexico between 1983 and 1987. The sharp increase in the DFI inflows in 1987 can be attributed to the debt-equity conversion that existed until November 1987 (when the Government terminated the program because of the inflationary impact of large scale debt-equity swaps); the "maquiladora" (in bond assembly) sector; and the *de-facto* relaxation of foreign investment regulations. Of the $3.88 billion DFI inflow that occurred in 1987, $1.85 billion were for debt-equity swaps involving public debt and $1.13 billion for private financial restructuring. About 1/4 of the total value of swaps in 1986 and 1987 was used to prepay debts owed to others by the local subsidiaries of foreign corporations in Mexico. Most of the direct foreign investment that has taken place in Mexico has been in the manufacturing sector (especially export-oriented manufacturing projects in industries, such as automobiles) and the services sector (especially the tourism industry).[11] This is not a coincidence given the fact that until recently foreigners were not permitted

Table 3.7
Breakdown of Foreign Investment in Mexico, 1983-87

	1983	1984	1985	1986	1987
		(US$ Millions)			
LONG-TERM CAPITAL					
Direct Foreign Investment	460.5	391.1	490.5	1,522.0	3,248.0
New Investment	70.2	543.4	269.6	944.0	2,386.3
Reinvested Profits	197.3	215.3	231.8	587.1	661.7
Net Receipts from Headquarters	193.0	(367.6)	(10.9)	(9.1)	200.0
Purchase of Firms	0.0	0.0	0.0	0.0	0.0
Other Liabilities of the Non-Bank Private Sector	545.6	386.5	(431.2)	(469.5)	(2,664.1)
Firms with Foreign Capital	295.2	293.2	(245.2)	(290.3)	(1,948.7)
Other Firms	250.4	93.3	(189.0)	(179.2)	(715.4)
Debt Renegotiation 1	2,558.4	0.0	0.0	(363.2)	(1,482.9)
SHORT-TERM CAPITAL					
Firms with Foreign Capital	(1,144.0)	(564.1)	(761.2)	(712.9)	(399.3)
Other Firms	(1,710.8)	(1,582.5)	(39.0)	(298.0)	26.3
Debt Renegotiation	(2,558.4)	0.0	0.0	0.0	0.0
Remitted Profits	184.0	241.0	386.3	335.0	385.2

( ) denotes a net payment abroad.
Source: Banco de Mexico, "Informe Annual," 1987 and "Indicadores Economicos," March 1988.
<u>Note</u>: 1. Debt renegotiation in 1983 represents rescheduling of short-term debt to long-term debt. In 1986-87, it represents debt-equity conversion.

Chart 3.5
Real DFI Flow into Mexico, 1973-87 (in 1987 U.S. dollars)

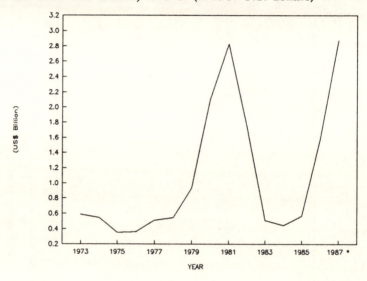

Chart 3.6
Share of DFI in GDP, 1973-87

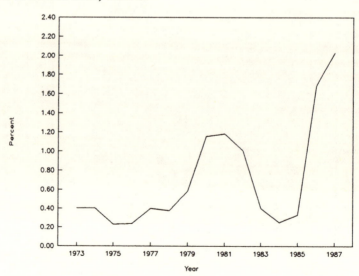

to invest in the agricultural sector and in public utilities. Most of the foreign investment into Mexico comes from investors in the United States.

Regulatory Restrictions on DFI in Mexico

The flow of direct foreign investment in Mexico is determined by three main factors: (1) macroeconomic policy and domestic regulations which affect the gross profitability of investment in Mexico; (2) regulations restricting the sectors, types of activities, and corporate structure in which foreign investment is allowed to enter the country; and (3) corporate tax laws, in general, and special tax rules that apply to foreign-owned/operated firms, in particular.

As far as the gross profitability of an investment is concerned, this factor is not peculiar to foreign investment. In general, foreign investment will react positively to the same policies that promote private investment by domestic investors in Mexico. In the last few years (1987-92), one of the major factors that has influenced foreigners to invest in Mexico, through its influence on the gross profitability of investment, has been the expected exchange rate at which they could exchange dollar-denominated Mexican external debt for local equity in conjunction with the debt-equity conversion program and privatization efforts of the Government.

There are several restrictions on foreign ownership established in the Mexican Constitution. The basic framework for DFI regulations was established in the *Foreign Investment Law of March 1973*. This law stipulates that foreigners have to obtain special permission from the Government in order to own more than 25 percent of any capital in Mexico. In addition, there are certain sectors of the economy from which foreign investment is completely prohibited and some where majority ownership cannot be in the hands of foreigners. The Mexican government has traditionally exercised tight control over foreign investors via legal and administrative channels, such as local content requirements, price controls, ceilings on foreign equity participation, tax concessions, import licensing, and access to foreign exchange at favorable rates. These regulations are implemented by the National Commission on Foreign Investment (CNIE), which is an interagency commission with the participation of all Government departments that have any connection to the subject. Specifically, CNIE is comprised of representatives from the secretariats of the interior, foreign affairs, treasury, labor, programming and budgeting, commerce and industrial development, and energy, mining, and Parastatal enterprises.

According to the 1973 Investment Law, prior CNIE approval is required when foreign investors seek ownership of 25 percent or more of capital or 49 percent or more of fixed assets of any enterprise in Mexico. Acquisition with over 25 percent foreign capital by foreign holding companies, or operations in which foreigners could determine management of the acquired firm (for example, if a foreign holding company purchases equity in a Mexican firm that is enough to result in net foreign ownership of 25 percent or more of all equity in that firm), also requires CNIE approval. New investment and expansion by existing foreign firms must also be sanctioned. In addition, the financing of new capital through capitalization or reinvested profits requires CNIE approval. Transfer of shares or assets among foreign investors requires no authorization as long as it does not involve debt capitalization or reinvested profits. Sale or transfer to other fully foreign-owned firms of the "maquiladora" sector with at least 75 percent foreign capital requires no authorization. Firms in the maquiladora sector may be fully foreign-owned. Secondary petrochemicals and auto parts industries are currently subject to a 40 percent ceiling on foreign equity participation.

CNIE approval by foreign investors is not the only encounter they are supposed to have with the Mexican authorities. Any foreigner who wants to invest in an enterprise in Mexico must also register at the National Register of Foreign Investment (RNIE). In general, every major foreign investment in Mexico requires a decision by the CNIE, and most of them need to be done on an *ad hoc* basis. It is often erroneously believed that Mexican law does not permit *any* foreign equity participation beyond the 49 percent maximum except in the maquiladora sector. In reality, the 1973 law gives CNIE the power to grant exceptions to the rules established by the 1973 law.

In the past, decisions by CNIE were said to take a long time and would involve tortuous bureaucratic procedures. This process created a great degree of discretionality and suspicion of rent-seeking activities by involved parties. This discretionality and the uncertainties associated with it have been cited as major impediments to larger inflows of foreign capital in the past. Since 1982, CNIE has been making every effort to reduce this degree of discretionality by setting standard rules by which decisions are made, and by communicating these rules to potential investors, investment banks, and legal and accounting firms representing foreign companies who wish to and are operating in Mexico.

In 1984, CNIE published a set of guidelines specifying those sectors in which the Government of Mexico wanted to encourage foreign direct investment, even as a majority owner. These priority sectors are:

- Nonelectrical machinery and equipment;
- Electrical machinery and appliances;

- Electronic equipment and accessories; and
- The tourism industry.

These sectors were perceived by the Government to have possible positive externalities associated with them that would benefit the Mexican economy. At the same time, the Government believed that Mexico had a comparative advantage in the production of these goods because of availability of raw materials, labor, and proximity to the U.S. markets.[12]

Changes in the DFI Regulations

The Government is taking steps to reduce the degree of discretionality in the approval process since 1986. In May 1987, a committee was set up to advise the Government on this issue. Its recommendations have been implemented, and the average response and approval time by CNIE of a foreign investment feasibility study has been reduced from an average of eight months to forty-five days. Certain types of expansion by foreign firms only require a notification to CNIE rather than prior approval from them. For some, investment approval by CNIE has become automatic. These include small and medium-sized manufacturing firms in the "maquiladora" sector that export, directly or indirectly, 35 percent of their output.

In February 1988, CNIE published a resolution that summarizes all the general rules and procedures related to foreign investment in Mexico, as well as all relevant regulations contained in recent laws passed by the Mexican Congress that modify this 1973 law. Major changes that have been made in the 1973 law include (1) new rules that make DFI in small and medium sized firms easier; (2) DFI coming from international development agencies (such as the International Finance Corporation) are given neutral status (i.e., not counted as foreign in determining the share of foreign capital in an enterprise); and (3) firms in the maquiladora sector producing only for exports are allowed 100 percent foreign ownership.

The system of DFI regulations is also becoming more transparent. CNIE has compiled a code containing all its past rulings. This will be available to potential investors who could assess their project with the precedents that have occurred and get an idea about whether the Government would be inclined to approve the project or not.

This liberalization of DFI regulations has coincided with the trade liberalization measures being pursued by the Mexican government after 1982. Increased DFI flows are being encouraged into sectors that will increase Mexico's non-oil export earnings. The ongoing process is also expected to make the industrial sector in Mexico more efficient and internationally competitive. Since 1982, the size of the maquiladora sector has more than doubled, both in terms of number of plants and in terms of value added by 1989.

In May 1989, DFI regulations were relaxed even further and were made more transparent. Specifically, majority foreign ownership of firms in the fishing, petrochemical, and mining sectors was permitted for the first time. The licensing of investments under $100 million was made automatic in these sectors. The approval of larger investments in these sectors became automatic after a forty-five-day waiting period, unless the Government provided a formal objection to the investor within the waiting period. The tax system has also been modified such that the marginal tax rates are close to levels in most major developed countries. This is expected to encourage the return of flight capital. In addition, for tax purposes, profits are adjusted for the effects of inflation on assets and liabilities.[13]

Debt Equity Conversion

The importance of the debt-equity conversion program in attracting foreign investment in Mexico in the recent past cannot be undermined. The sharp increase in DFI flows between 1986-87 can be attributed to the debt-equity conversion program. This is illustrated by the fact that the sectoral distribution of DFI inflows between 1986-87 is almost identical (in percentage terms) to those resulting from the debt-equity conversions in Mexico. Twenty-five percent of the total value of debt-equity swaps carried out during the period 1986-87 was used to repay debt owed to others by the local subsidiaries of foreign multinationals in Mexico. Only a part of this amount can be regarded as truly "additional" capital formation. Prior to 1985, subsidiaries of foreign firms financed a large proportion of their operations with local borrowing. However, after domestic real interest rates began to rise in Mexico, these highly leveraged capital structures were too costly for the firms to maintain. Debt-equity swaps provided them with an avenue to repay this debt in a relatively inexpensive manner.[14]

The debt-equity program was suspended in November 1987 on the grounds that it was generating inflationary pressures on the economy. The Government believed that the massive conversions of dollar debt into peso investments would fuel an expansion in money supply and rekindle the hyperinflation crisis. It was also believed to be disadvantageous to the foreign investors who had entered the Mexican market prior to the establishment of the debt-equity conversion program, because they were unable to reap the substantial gain from debt conversions in order to finance their investments.

The debt-equity conversion program involving the conversion of public debt to private equity was reopened in August 1988 to consider the backlog of proposals that were in the approval process at the time of the November 1987 suspensions. No new applications were being accepted. Given the fact that conversions of *private* debt for *private* equity are not inflationary, debt-equity swaps involving private debt have not been discontinued.[15]

The current president has indicated, however, that future new authorizations may be limited solely to priority projects, such as those in "tourism corridors," and even there it may not be available for projects in attractive tourist spots, like Puerto Vallarta and Cancun, where foreigners would invest anyway. Debt-equity conversions would be a good channel for achieving success in Mexico's privatization program, where some of the private enterprises, in themselves, would not be productive or profitable enough for private foreign investors to be forthcoming. The availability of truly "additional" direct foreign investment (i.e., that which would not have occurred without these additional incentives from the Government) will, of course, depend on the new tax laws and ongoing Pact for Stabilization and Growth (PECE), on the operations of firms with foreign participation and on their expectations for the future course of the Mexican economy.

As for debt-equity swaps involving *public* debt for *private* equity, large-scale conversions will have an inflationary impact on the economy, the reason being that in order to execute this type of debt-equity conversion, the Government has to raise resources to acquire the private asset. The inflationary impact of this exercise will depend on how these resources are raised. The Government can increase its primary budget surplus, increase money supply (the inflation tax), issue internal debt or increase external debt, or incur international reserve losses.

Given the stringent adjustment measures currently being pursued by the Government in Mexico, the public sector surplus cannot be increased (or public sector deficit cannot be cut further). Increasing money supply will have a direct inflationary impact, which is precisely what the Government is trying to avoid. Issuing internal debt will lead to a further pressure on the public sector's budget because of the interest payments on this domestic debt. Use of international reserves is impossible under the acute foreign exchange constraints faced by Mexico. Finally, increasing external debt further will increase its debt burden, which is precisely what the Government is trying to deal with via the debt-equity conversion program. Only in the case of a privatization program, where the Government already owns the assets that it wishes to convert to private equity via the debt-equity

Chart 3.7
Sectoral Distribution of DFI, 1987

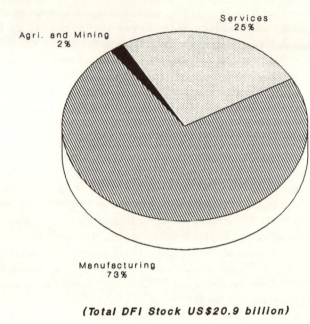

Services
25%

Agri. and Mining
2%

Manufacturing
73%

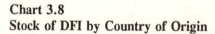

(Total DFI Stock US$20.9 billion)

Source: Banco de Mexico

Chart 3.8
Stock of DFI by Country of Origin

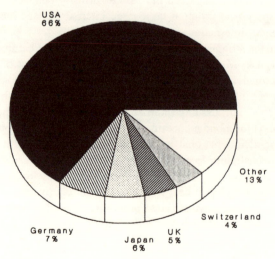

USA
66%

Other
13%

Switzerland
4%

Germany
7%

Japan
6%

UK
5%

Source: Banco de Mexico

swap program, will the problem of inflation not be encountered.

Several governments, like Mexico, are therefore only permitting debt-equity swaps involving *private* debt and are evaluating the feasibility of privatization of large public sector enterprises in conjunction with a debt-equity conversion program. Nevertheless, it should be noted that the issue of privatization of existing public sector enterprises is by no means an easy task because of the social and political considerations, as well as the issue of sovereignty that is associated with this endeavor.

Another possibility for direct foreign investment in Mexico is through portfolio investment via the Mexican Stock Exchange. Currently, however, the scope of large-scale portfolio investment in Mexico is somewhat limited.[16]

THE ROAD TOWARDS REDUCING ITS DEBT OVERHANG

After having looked at the effort that the Mexican Government has made in bringing about structural changes in its economy in the face of several short-run difficulties and in attracting direct foreign investment (in conjunction with its trade liberalization efforts), we now proceed to discuss the dealings of Mexico with its external creditors. Since most of Mexico's external debt is owed to private creditors, we will focus our attention on Mexico's relationship with its commercial bank creditors.

Cooperation by Mexico's private creditors is indispensable to bringing about an orderly settlement of its debt-servicing difficulties. It is in this line of reasoning that Mexico has been able to initiate most of the significant developments in the global strategy for dealing with the International Debt Crisis.

In the context of Mexico's role in bringing the International Debt Crisis to the forefront, Katz (1989) has stated: Although Mexico was not the first developing country faced with default, it was the first one in which the international banking system had a great deal at stake [Katz (1989)]. So, after Mexico declared a moratorium on debt service payments in August 1982 and temporary bridge loans were arranged under the auspices of the U.S. government and the BIS, the commercial bank debt restructuring package for dealing with this crisis had to be hammered out. Given the number of private creditors who were involved in the case of Mexico, it was not feasible for the Government to deal with them on a one-to-one basis. In the case of official creditors, the mechanism of the Paris Club existed. In 1982, no such mechanism existed for private creditors [Katz (1989)]. According to Joseph Kraft (1984), when Mexico's private creditors assembled in New York after August 1982, there were about 800. So in order to deal with the problem, a Bank Advisory Committee (BAC) was set up, consisting of fourteen members representing leading banks in the United States, Europe, and Japan. Each U.S. bank represented ten regional banks that, in turn, represented smaller local banks. A similar pyramid structure was applied to the other representatives of the BAC. It was this BAC that was then given the task of dealing with Mexican officials in negotiating an appropriate debt restructuring package.

After lengthy negotiations between the BAC and the Mexican government and the finalization of a three-year IMF adjustment program (i.e., the National Development Plan, which was discussed earlier), an agreement was signed between the commercial banks and the Mexican Government wherein Mexico received $5 billion in new loans to be repaid in six years, with three years' grace at a spread of 2-1/2 percentage points above LIBOR in addition to an upfront fee of 1-1/4 percent. The new loans amounted to about 7 percent of each bank's exposure in Mexico. Also, $20 billion in short-term loans that were due in August 1982 were rescheduled so as to be paid in eight years with four years' grace at a spread of 1-7/8 percentage points over LIBOR along with a 1 percent upfront fee.

The strategy that seems to have been adopted was one of buying time. During this time, it was expected that Mexico's export earnings would increase, and the fruits of the adjustment process would be observed. It also gave banks the time to reduce their exposure in developing countries and reorganize their own portfolios so as to reduce the vulnerability of their earnings (and, hence, profits), which resulted from such shocks. Given the fees that were charged, the so-called Mexican "Rescue package" was, indeed, profitable for the banks. At the same time, the spreads charged on rescheduled Mexican loans were the lowest rates granted by banks to any country at that time.

With the successful implementation of the economic adjustment program in 1983, Mexico was making timely interest payments. Yet, in 1984, it needed $3.8 billion in new loans to deal with the bunching of repayments and desired a further rescheduling of existing claims. Given the stringent adjustment effort and the support of the multilateral agencies, Mexico was easily able to acquire additional loans from its commercial bank creditors, once again at the best possible terms granted to any developing country at that time. Under the comprehensive debt restructuring package that was worked out for 1984-85, a total of $48.5 billion in outstanding claims of commercial bank, including $20 billion that were previously rescheduled and the $5 billion new loan it had received in 1983, were rescheduled with a fourteen-year maturity and a lower spread of 1-1/8 percent over LIBOR. In addition, this debt restructuring agreement allowed banks the option of converting a portion of their dollar-denominated debt into their own national currency. No fees were charged by the banks under this rescheduling agreement, once again a first among developing country debtors.

These multiple reschedulings and new borrowings that took place were merely providing Mexico temporary cash flow relief in the short run. The postponement of repayments of principal did not preclude the fact that between 1983-85 Mexico continued to meet its scheduled interest payments in full. Net transfers from commercial bank creditors were in fact negative, implying that more was being taken out of the economy than was being put in. This took place at a time when Mexico was following a policy of extreme public sector retrenchment with the public budget being reduced by the maximum possible extent.

In 1986, when the oil prices declined and Mexico's export earnings declined drastically, fiscal restraint was not the answer to its debt-servicing difficulties. The Government had reduced public investment and drastically devalued the peso (in nominal terms). It negotiated a $500 million bridge loan to tide it over its difficulties while it came to the negotiating table, once again with its commercial bank creditors.

At this time, the "Baker Plan" was being discussed as a way of dealing with the debt-servicing problems of LDCs. Mexico was one of the first countries to obtain new loans under the auspices of the Baker Initiative. The debt restructuring agreement that was signed between the BAC and the Government was unique in several ways: It was not only linked to loans from the World Bank ($500 million) and an IMF adjustment program, but, for the first time, the IMF agreed to provide $600 million in case the oil price fell below $9 per barrel. Two contingency funds were set up with the commercial banks wherein $1.2 billion in new loans would automatically be available to Mexico if the growth targets of the first quarter of 1987 were not attained. In addition, the IMF set a precondition for this debt restructuring agreement to be supported by them--that $6 billion in new loans (medium-and long-term) be made by banks to Mexico. The new loans and rescheduled obligations from commercial banks carried a lower spread of 13/16 percent over the six-month LIBOR.

In the context of the stringent adjustment carried out by Mexico between 1982 and 1988, Sweder van Wijnbergen has stated:

Despite the far reaching reforms implemented in Mexico, international capital markets have not provided the resources needed to bridge the period between the current costs and the future benefits of the reform program. The continuing high external transfers generated uncertainly about whether the rapidly growing transfer burden could be met. This, in turn, generated increased uncertainly about future exchange rates, taxation and financial regulation. Thus, to forestall further capital flight, Mexico had to pay unsustainable interest rates on its domestic debt. [van Wijnbergen (1990), p. 6]

THE AZTEC BOND

Given this situation in early 1988, the Mexican government decided to endeavor to reduce the stock of debt outstanding in order to reduce its debt service burden in the long run, improve expectations among private savers and investors in Mexico, and, in turn, bring about growth. Mexico engaged reputable U.S. investment banking firms to tender proposals by which it could reduce its stock of debt outstanding to external creditors by taking advantage of the secondary market discount for Mexican debt that prevailed at the time. The strategy Mexico chose to adopt was a "voluntary debt exchange," a method frequently adopted by U.S. firms in order to match their contractual debt service profile more closely with their current and anticipated cash flows. Once again, this was a first in the international debt arena.

Since this type of mechanism had not been tried by a debtor country on a large scale before, Mexico began to test the waters with an announcement that it was prepared to issue up to $10 billion in a new negotiable bond (the "Aztec Bond") that had a twenty-year bullet maturity.[17] This bond would be exchanged for rescheduled debt owed to its commercial bank creditors. The interest rate on these bonds would be 1-5/8 percentage points over the six-month LIBOR. This was double the rate charged on the rescheduled debt. In addition, the principal of the new bond is fully collateralized with twenty-year zero-coupon bonds issued by the U.S. Treasury. The rate at which the old debt was exchanged for the new bonds was determined by an auction in which banks submitted tenders specifying the discount at which a dollar's worth of the old restructure loans would be exchanged for the new bonds and the total amount they would make available for the purpose.

The Aztec Bonds are listed in the Luxembourg Stock Exchange and are traded internationally through the Eurobond market. In accordance with normal practices for Euromarket transactions, these bonds can be traded only at the private placement market in the United States. The issue cannot be registered with the Securities and Exchange Commission (SEC) under the Securities Act of the U.S. Constitution. This implies that these bonds cannot be publicly offered or traded in the United States.

The collateral on these bonds is held in an escrow account at the Federal Reserve Bank of New York in the form of a book entry. The exact amount of this collateral has been determined by the volume and price of the old restructured debt that was exchanged and the market interest rate prevailing at the time.

All the debt that was included in the 1985 commercial bank debt restructuring and the 1983-84 restructuring agreements was eligible for the exchange (a total of about $53 billion). The new loans that Mexico had received in 1986-87 along with Mexico's short-term debt and debt owed by the private sector were not eligible for this exchange offer.

Since Mexico had signed restructuring agreements with the commercial banks before, it was obligated to obtain waivers from a majority of the banks on the *sharing clauses* relating to prepayment of loans, the *pari passu clauses* relating to the order of payment to creditors, and the *negative pledge clauses* provided in the existing agreements. The negative pledge clauses contained in Mexico's agreements with the World Bank and the Inter-American Development Bank were also waived. Mexico also had to be provided similar collateral enhancement on other existing Mexican bonds because of the negative pledge clauses incorporated in these bonds. (This is said to have caused Mexico an additional cost of $100 million.)

These bonds are "senior" to the old restructured debt in that they contain a pari passu clause that allows them to be treated on similar terms as all other external debt, including obligations to multilateral organizations, such as the World Bank and the International Monetary Fund. However, these bonds have call provisions whereby they could be amortized earlier than scheduled at the discretion of the Mexican authorities.

At the close of the auction on February 26, 1988, 139 banks had submitted tenders offering a total of $6.7 billion in eligible debt for exchange. The highest bid ratio (i.e., amount of old eligible debt to be exchanged per dollar of the new bonds) was $2.08, and the lowest was $1.121. Most of the offers had a bid ratio between $1.44 and $1.54 of old debt per dollar of new bonds. The difference in bid ratios can be explained by the differences in perception of the banks on the "seniority" of the bonds and on the expectations about the behavior of the secondary market price for old restructured Mexican debt *after* the exchange.

The Mexican authorities ranked the bids in descending order of bid ratio and moved down the list until it reached its reservation bid ratio of $1.33 of old debt per dollar of new bonds and purchased debt at the bank's bid ratio. This enabled Mexico to maximize the amount of eligible debt exchanged. Mexico accepted the bids from ninety-five banks for $3.7

billion in debt. Japanese banks offered the largest amount followed by the U.S. and Canadian banks. However, it is important to note that of the thirty U.S. banks that submitted bids, only two or three large money-center banks participated in the exchange.

$2.6 billion in new bonds were issued at an average exchange ratio of $1.42 of old restructured debt per dollar of the new bond. The stock of Mexico's external debt owed to commercial banks was reduced by $1.1 billion. Interest savings of $600 million per year were achieved from this exchange. Folkerts-Landau and Rodriguez (1989) have stated that:

> The Mexican proposal may be regarded as the first step toward the system of development finance that existed before the 1930's, that is, development finance being provided through a broad-based bond market at risk-related yields, while collateralized trade finance is being provided by banks. [Folkerts-Landau and Rodriguez (1989) p. 370]

However, from Mexico's point of view, this exchange offer was not a success, since it could only exchange $3.7 billion of old restructured loans for the new bonds instead of the $10 billion it had desired to exchange. Folkerts-Landau and Rodriguez (1989) have used an asset-pricing model to show that if Mexico had been successful in exchanging a larger volume of bids at the average exchange ratio of old bank debt for new bonds, the exchange offer would have been equivalent to a direct cash buyback at the prevailing secondary market price for Mexican debt ($0.50 per dollar) at that time.

The Mexican bond offer was a precursor to the latest debt reduction package that was negotiated between Mexico and its commercial bank creditors under the "Brady Initiative."

THE 1989-90 DEBT REDUCTION PACKAGE

By early 1989, the need for debt reduction for Mexico was accepted by all involved parties. Between 1982-88 the situation in Mexico was not very much better than it was in August 1982, when it was instrumental in bringing the International Debt Crisis to the forefront. There had been no GDP growth over the period; standards of living had fallen; the infrastructure had deteriorated as a result of the reduced public expenditure and private investment; inflation had again become rampant; capital flight was beginning to occur; and the domestic interest rates were at unsustainably high levels. Investor confidence was at a low ebb. The

burden of debt was having a negative effect on the incentive of the people
to save and invest.

In the international arena, several debt reduction proposals were being
discussed (as explained in Chapter 1) of which the Brady Initiative was
gaining importance. Official support for debt reduction came in the form
of special funds being earmarked from the World Bank and the International
Monetary Fund for this purpose. The appropriate mechanism for bringing
about debt reduction had to be determined.

Mexico was, once again, one of the first HICs to negotiate a
comprehensive debt restructuring package under the auspices of the Brady
Initiative. Unlike the previous debt reduction operation (the Aztec Bond
offer) that had been carried out the previous year, the current DDSR
package had to be comprehensive (involving *all* commercial bank creditors,
i.e., no free riders) and had to provide both short-term cash flow relief as
well as lower debt service payments over the medium term. The DDSR
package had to be a *negotiated* settlement of Mexico's debt problems, since
Mexico did not want to follow a confrontational approach on the basis of
its own long-term interest of eventually entering the voluntary capital
markets. This was also welcomed by the international financial community,
which was aware of the stringent adjustment policies Mexico had been
pursuing and the deteriorating domestic conditions in spite of such efforts.

Debt reduction would reduce the debt overhang, which would reduce
the prevailing uncertainties regarding future exchange rate and fiscal and
monetary policy of the Government. This would improve the expectations
of private investors regarding their expected future returns on their
investment so as to increase investment and, eventually, bring about growth.
In addition, the fiscal situation of the Government would improve because
of the lower transfers of resources abroad in the form of debt service
payments.

Van Wijnbergen (1990) has contended that:

Mexico had the structural policies and domestic fiscal measures in place
for sustainable growth to take off. What was missing was a sufficiently
long period during which external creditors would allow this inherently
sound economic program to get off the ground. The only way of
obtaining a credible commitment to such medium term international
accommodation is debt relief. [van Wijnbergen (1990)]

Chart 3.9 shows the structure of Mexico's external debt obligations,
and Chart 3.10 shows the composition of Mexico's external creditors as of
December 1987.

At the end of 1988, Mexico owed $100.4 billion to its external creditors, of which $70.6 billion were owed to commercial banks. Medium-and long-term commercial bank debt of $52.7 billion was eligible for the 1989-90 DDSR operation.[18]

On July 23, 1989, Mexico reached an agreement with its Bank Advisory Committee on a DDSR package. This package consists of three options of the market-based menu:

- *A Discount Swap*: Banks can choose to exchange eligible debt for a thirty-year bond at 35 percent discount on the face value of the old debt. This bond will pay interest with a spread of 13/16th percentage points over LIBOR;
- *A Par Swap*: Banks can choose to exchange eligible debt for a thirty-year bond at no discount on the face value of the old debt. This bond will pay a fixed below market interest rate of 6.25 percent per annum (or its equivalent in the case of non dollar denominated debt); and
- *New Money Commitment*: Additional loans equivalent to 7 percent of the principal balance at the conclusion of the agreement and 6 percent in 1990, 1991, and 1992 at a spread of 13/16th percentage points over LIBOR.

The two bonds will have their principal collateralized by thirty-year zero-coupon bonds of the U.S. Treasury (or its equivalent in the case of other currencies). In addition, the bonds will not be subject to sharing clauses, which have been a part of previous syndicated loan agreements. This has been done to deal with the problem of banks that choose to be free-riders to the agreement; for example, banks that do not participate in this DDSR operation and exchange their old claims on Mexico for the bonds would not be legally able to share equally in any payments Mexico makes on its restructured debt.

Another ingredient of the current agreement is the inclusion of a *recapture clause* which stipulates that in the event of an increase in oil prices by a certain percentage *in 1997 and beyond,* the banks would share in the increased revenue. There is, however, a cap on the maximum amount of additional payments Mexico would have to make in case the oil price rose in 1997 onwards, which is equal to 3 percent of the amount of debt exchanged for the two bonds. There is also a contingency financing facility arrangement from the banks in case the oil price falls below certain levels. Up to $400 million would also be available from the IMF under the Compensatory and Contingency Financing Facility arrangements.

Chart 3.9
Structure of External Debt, 1987

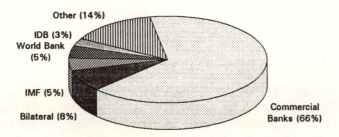

(Total External Debt: $107.45 billion)

Chart 3.10
Composition of External Debt, 1987

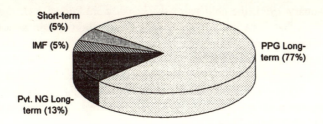

The two bonds will also carry between 1-1/2 to two years of interest payments guaranteed on a rolling basis through an escrow account. Funds for this account are being provided by the World Bank, the IMF, the Government of Japan and from Mexico's own resources. These bonds are excluded from future new money calls by Mexico, are non reschedulable, and are, therefore, senior to the old debt obligations and preferred by banks who would not want to be part of any concerted new money operation in the future.

The banks will also be allowed to relend, up to a maximum limit specified in the agreement, their claims to public enterprises in Mexico. In addition, banks that had given Mexico debt relief would qualify to participate in a debt-equity swap program of at most $1 billion a year.

A total of $7 billion in resources are to be provided for all the collaterals and enhancements on this DDSR package. Apart from the financing that will come from the IMF and the World Bank, $5.3 billion will come from Japan through a cofinancing operation, and $1.7 billion will come from Mexico's own reserves.[19]

Given the tax, regulatory, and accounting practices in the creditor countries, the Discount Swap will most likely be preferred by regional banks in the United States with strong reserve positions, such as Security Pacific and First Chicago. The Par Swap, on the other hand, would most likely be preferred by the U.S. money center banks, since it avoids the need to write down the face value of loans. The New Money Commitment option is geared towards banks that, because of to their long-term business interests in the region, concerns about precedence setting and other factors, are vehemently opposed to debt forgiveness in general. (Citicorp is a case in point).

In January 1990, the choices of the banks were known. Of the total $52.7 billion that were initially tendered, $48.4 billion remain as a result of debt-equity swaps, cross-country exchange rate changes, and the cancellation of debt held by Mexican institutions that occurred between 1988-89. Of the $48.4 billion that are covered under the new restructuring agreement, 40 percent of the banks chose the discount bonds (principal reduction), 49 percent chose the par bonds (interest reduction), and the remaining would provide new money.

From the banks' point of view, this debt reduction package has lowered their "balance sheet risk" by the collateralization of principal with zero-coupon bonds. In this way, banks will effectively be insured for 100 percent of principal by the IRS (in the case of U.S. banks). Loan loss reserves are generally needed to protect against losses on principal. So, because of the collateralization of the principal, the banks do not need to back these claims on Mexico, and these reserves can then be used for other purposes by the banks. Therefore, there is less pressure on the money center banks to raise reserves, issue common stock, or cut earnings of existing shareholders.

Since the bonds are collateralized and interest payments partly guaranteed, the risk of default by Mexico has been lowered. Mexico's payments are lower because of the lower stock of debt and lower interest rate on the par bonds. This the banks' would perceive as a lowering of their default risk.

From Mexico's point of view, it has benefited by obtaining a medium-term agreement that provides both cash flow relief in the short run (in terms of lower interest payments and no principal payments until year thirty on the bonds), as well as a reduction in the stock of debt (which translates into lowering of the debt overhang).

As long as Mexico continues to service its remaining debt, the funds deposited in the escrow account (for interest guarantee) and the collateral (U.S. Treasury bonds) will earn interest that will accrue to Mexico. From these interest earnings the additional debt service payments Mexico has to make on the loans it received from the World Bank, IMF, and Japan, as well as the opportunity cost of its own reserves used for the DDSR operation, should be subtracted to obtain the net benefit to Mexico from this package.

As for the effect of reducing the debt overhang towards improving confidence within Mexico and increasing private investment and savings, it is too early to say anything decisive at this point. It should be noted, however, that the *ex-post* real interest rates that were almost 50 percent in the weeks prior to the debt accord fell immediately after the deal was announced. Nominal interest rates fell from 56 percent to around 36 percent immediately after the DDSR agreement was announced.[20] This observation can be explained by the fact that the DDSR agreement reduced Mexico's debt service obligations, which means reduced net transfers abroad by the Mexican government. This implies reduced pressure on the exchange rate and the public sector budget. Since the deal is medium term in nature, lower external transfers imply reduced uncertainty about future taxation, financial regulation, and exchange rates. The risk associated with peso-denominated public debt is reduced, and, in turn, domestic interest rates should decline. Whether this decline in domestic interest rates will be sustainable and will translate into increased investment and growth in Mexico cannot be concluded at this time.

NOTES

1. Max Cordon (1984) has termed this situation as a "Dutch Disease."

2. See "Mexico: Development Financing Strategy, 1986c," SHCP and "Mexico: Main Economic Issues," SHCP (1986e) for details on the National Development Plan (1983-85) and the "Programa de Alientoy Credimiento" (PAC) of 1986.

3. Source: Secretaria de Hacienda y Credito Publico (SHCP).

4. Imports controls were somewhat liberalized in 1984-85 and imports grew in 1985-87.

5. Source: SHCP "Mexico: Development Financing Strategy, 1986c," p. 24.

6. Source: SHCP (1986c).

7. See van Wijnbergen (1990) for details on the developments in Mexico during 1988-90.

8. Source: van Wijnbergen (1989), pp. 4-5.

9. Most of the material for this section has been taken from Sudarshan Gooptu (1989c), "Direct Foreign Investment in Mexico," *World Bank CFS Informal Financial Notes Series*, No. 6, March 1989.

10. These figures are cumulative totals of actual DFI inflows in current U.S. dollars and may be biased because of the inflationary changes that took place between the years. Source: Banco de Mexico, "The Mexican Economy," 1988, p. 132.

11. Source: Commission Nacional de Inversion Extranjera (CNIE), Mexico D.F.

12. See Gooptu (1989c), for a summary of the regulations, restrictions, and tax obligations and incentives associated with direct foreign investment in Mexico.

13. Source: van Wijnbergen (1990) p. 5.

14. See Joel Bergsman and Wayne Edisis (1988) for details on debt equity conversions in Latin America, in general, and in Mexico, in particular. The issue of "additionality" of investment via debt equity conversions is also addressed here in greater detail.

15. See Ruben Lamdany (1988a) for details on the inflationary impact on debt-equity conversions.

16. Appendix C of this book provides a description of the Mexican Stock Exchange and assesses the feasibility of portfolio investment by foreigners.

17. *Bullet maturity* is defined as a one-time payment of principal of the bond at maturity.

18. Source: World Bank, "World Debt Tables," 1989-90, Vol. 1, pp. 52-53.

19. Source: World Bank, 1990

20. van Wijnbergen (1990), p. 28.

4

The Mechanics of a Growth-oriented
Debt Reduction Strategy:
A Theoretical Exposition

From the general overview of the International Debt Crisis that was provided in the earlier chapters, along with a detailed discussion of the Mexican case, it is quite clear that the situation of the HICs has not changed significantly since the International Debt Crisis came to the forefront in 1982, when Mexico declared a moratorium on debt service payments to its commercial bank creditors. As discussed in the previous chapters, several countries (of which, Mexico is a prime example) have had to generate significant trade and savings surpluses at the expense of consumption and domestic investment.

The results of the stringent economic adjustment measures in these countries have been mixed. The improvement in the trade balances of these countries has been achieved mainly through a drastic reduction in imports rather than an increase in exports. In addition, countries producing primary goods have faced a reduction in the prices of their exportables in the international markets, which has contributed to the pressure they face to reduce imports further and increase the volume of exports in order to generate enough resources to meet their contractual debt service obligations. Consequently, there has been almost no increase in GDP and per capita consumption in most countries. The proponents of some of the proposals put forward to "solve" the debt crisis believed that in the long run, a country could grow out of its Debt Problem by generating the necessary surpluses through increases in exports and in domestic savings. In the interim, new loans would be provided to tide the HIC over its hard times. The Baker Plan was based on this very premise.

What is crucial here is the fact that the longer the time period over which adjustment has to take place before any significant gains are observed, in terms of increased output and higher trade surpluses, the more uncertainty one has to face about the behavior of the factors that influence the very sustainability of the adjustment process. The greater the number of factors one has to consider, the more complex the task becomes for policy makers to monitor the progress of the economy towards successful adjustment and growth.

As the situation stands today, most of the highly indebted countries continue to face a situation of a debt overhang, which is influencing the incentives of domestic investors to invest in these countries for fear that the returns from these investment projects would find their way into the hands of external creditors. A strategy of debt reduction is emerging as a way of dealing with this debt overhang problem, thereby expecting to bring about investment and growth in these highly indebted countries.

In this chapter, a brief survey of the theoretical literature on the International Debt Crisis is provided in which the major issues that are in the frontier of research on international debt are highlighted. Thereafter, a theoretical model is formulated to show that there exists an optimal level of investment in an economy facing a situation of a debt overhang (i.e., a country on the wrong side of the "Debt-Laffer Curve", à la Jeffrey Sachs [1988]), after its creditors grant it some amount of debt relief so as to reduce the stock of the country's debt below a threshold level.

Since all external creditors cannot simply write down their loans to these HICs the debt relief that has to be granted by them has to be attained through the use of a market-based menu of options. In this chapter, an analytical framework is then presented to evaluate the gains to the debtor nation from embarking on a buy back of its external debt at a discount quoted on the secondary market for LDC debt, as opposed to a concessional rescheduling of existing claims of the commercial banks. The implications of using different sources of financing for the buyback are specifically incorporated into the model. Reduced-form equations for the Present Value of Debt Service relief under different scenarios of financing for the buyback are derived. In the next chapter, the results of the model are examined for the Mexican case.

THEORETICAL ANALYSES IN THE CONTEXT OF THE DEBT CRISIS: A SURVEY OF THE LITERATURE

In recent years, there have been three major developments in the context of Third World debt that have been occupying the minds in the profession. Broadly speaking, these are:

1. The "Debt-Laffer Curve" argument (P. Krugman [1988a]), which, simply put, says that debt repayment may be viewed as a tax imposed by external creditors. If the stock of debt outstanding of a country is large enough to cause a severe debt burden on the debtor country, it will not have any incentive to improve its well-being in order to repay its debt. By granting debt relief and, hence, lowering the stock of debt below the critical level, creditors would improve their chances of being repaid and, in turn, of increasing their revenues.

2. The diversity of external creditors precludes the possibility of using a single option for reducing a debtor country's external debt obligations (with tax, accounting, and regulatory factors along with the long- term business interests of banks in a particular region playing a key role). This results in the need to devise debt restructuring "packages," consisting of different market-based menu options, such as new money, cash buybacks, and debt-equity swaps, among others.

3. The increasing importance of the secondary market price in debt renegotiations between a debtor country and its commercial banks has led to an urgent preoccupation in the profession with devising models that forecast the secondary market price of a country's debt.

Numerous studies have also been conducted to examine the external and internal dynamics of foreign debt.[1] Mario Simonsen (1988) has shown that the relationship among debt, foreign exchange earnings, and the interest rate can be reduced to the relationship between the rate of growth of exports and the international interest rate. Another important observation in this context has been put forward by M. Selowsky and H. G. van Der Tak (1986), wherein they have shown that the outcome of a growth-oriented debt strategy hinges critically on the growth rate of domestic savings, and on the relationship between consumption and GDP growth in the debtor country. Sweder van Wijnbergen (1988, 1989) has highlighted the relationship between external debt and internal debt by focusing on a Government budget constraint that includes the activities of the Central Bank. However, his model does not provide the Government with a tool to set policy variables, such that a particular social welfare function is maximized. Nevertheless, it does allow us to evaluate the consistency between fiscal deficits and other macroeconomic targets in the debtor country.

In recent discussions on the behavior of an economy that is faced with a debt overhang, the debate about "liquidity versus solvency" of a country has been put to rest. It has been argued in the past that new lending should be provided to cover debt service payments in the countries with a liquidity problem and not those with a solvency problem. Krugman has stated that "liquidity crises must occur because of doubts about solvency" [Krugman (1988a), p. 258]. When a country is perceived, by external creditors, to be able to repay the full present value of its debt (or even a significant proportion of it), it could attract voluntary loans from banks by offering sufficiently high interest rates. Krugman has suggested that the expectation of insolvency does not prevent new lending from being in the interest of the country's *existing* creditors. That is to say that a debt restructuring package may consist of a "new money" component, if it ensures that existing creditors would receive the full present value of the country's potential resource transfer (which is more than they would have received without this new lending).

In the context of the theoretical developments in the analysis of the International Debt Crisis, Krugman has quite rightly stated:

> While there is a fairly substantial theoretical literature on the problem of sovereign risk (surveyed by Eaton et al. [1986]), the bulk of this literature has focussed either on the case of creditor rationing of a country that is borrowing with no existing debt, or the choice by a country whether to repay or default. The position in the real world, however, is one of both repayment and new borrowing; countries have arrived in the current situation with a stock of "inherited" debt, which they cannot fully service without new borrowing. [Krugman (1988a) pp. 253-254]

Theoretical analyses of this debt overhang problem are only recently beginning to emerge with papers by Sachs (1985), Krugman (1988), Kenneth Froot (1989), Stijn Claessens and Ishac Diwan (1990), and Daniel Cohen (1990).

It has been argued that in the presence of a debt overhang, countries should default on their loans owed to external creditors instead of reaching a negotiated settlement of their external debt problem--be it through rescheduling and/or debt reduction. Empirical evidence (World Bank, "World Debt Tables," 1989-90) suggests that between 1983 and 1989, net transfers from private creditors (i.e., commercial banks and suppliers) have been *negative*, thereby implying that countries have, indeed, made large payments to their external creditors, instead of declaring a permanent moratorium. Michael Dooley and Lars Svensson (1990) have argued that a Government cannot declare a permanent moratorium on debt service payments because of the inherent incentive that it would have to resume payments once the country's economic situation improved. Specifically, they put forth the hypothesis that if a Government did declare a permanent suspension of debt service payments owed to external creditors, which was perceived by investors to be so, then investment would increase. The permanent default would send a signal that new investors would not be taxed in the future to pay existing creditors. However, in the absence of a negotiated settlement with its external creditors, these creditors would continue to hold the debt and accumulate arrears. Moratorium interest would then be added to these arrears, so that the debtor country's contractual obligations would grow over time. Given this fact, the "permanent" default would inevitably become "temporary" after a rise in investment and income in the debtor country. It would be optimal for the debtor country to resume debt service payments, because the marginal costs of resuming payments would be lower than the benefits to the country from avoiding penalties resulting from the moratorium.[2] This incentive to resume payments would be enhanced because of the adverse effects of the moratorium on the availability and cost of short-term trade lines (which are mainly provided from private sources). This need for short-term trade lines would become especially important when necessary consumer and spare parts have to be imported in the presence of a liquidity crisis in the debtor country.[3]

Following this train of thought, it would be inevitable for a debtor country to try to reach a *negotiated settlement* of its Debt Problem before unilaterally declaring a permanent moratorium on debt service payments. Under these circumstances, the declaration of a permanent moratorium, after a sincere effort on the part of the debtor to reach a negotiated settlement, would be more credible to investors, and the anticipated increases in investment and, hence, growth would occur. If, in the course of a negotiated settlement, the stock of debt outstanding is reduced, the effect on investment will be similar.

Arriving at a negotiated settlement of a country's Debt Problem is by no means a simple task. Given the large number of commercial banks involved in most HICs a "package" consisting of a market-based menu of options is often negotiated with the banks being represented by a Bank Steering Committee. The options adopted in the package are greatly influenced by tax, regulatory, and accounting considerations of the banks and their long-term business interests in a region. The latter has become especially true now compared to the 1980s, after banks have systematically reduced their LDC exposure and set aside loan-loss provisions for problem loans. Some banks (e.g., Citicorp) have gone to the extent of freezing overseas assets of a country that did not meet its debt service obligations. The issue of precedence is also an important consideration in determining which option in the package the banks would adopt.[4]

The secondary market price (SMP) of a country's debt is crucial in the context of debt reduction. It has played a vital role in determining the price at which a buyback will occur. Studies by Sebastian Edwards (1986), Michael Dooley (1987), Jeffrey Sachs and Harry Huizinga (1987), Ruben Lamdany (1988), Silvina Vatnick (1988), John Purcell and Diego Orlanski (1989), and Stijn Claessens and Sweder van Wijnbergen (1989) have made significant contributions in increasing our understanding of how the secondary market price is determined. An important observation about secondary market prices in the context of a debt reduction operation is the fact that there are a variety of actions a *debtor* country can take to affect their future ability to make resource transfers, for example, exchange rate adjustment, investment, budget policies, and so forth. In addition, the secondary market for developing country debt is "thin," in the sense that the number of agents on the supply and demand sides of the market is small. This will then trickle down to the secondary market price for its debt. Because of this "moral hazard" problem, countries may have the incentive to stop making debt service payments in order to reduce the SMP of their debt and then proceed to buy back their debt at a discount. This effect will strengthen the negative incentive towards investment in countries that are faced with a debt overhang, hence, the need for a negotiated settlement of its Debt Problem.

Krugman (1988a) has stated that the secondary market discount is just another aspect of the fact that new lending is unprofitable when viewed in isolation, but it may be deemed essential by existing creditors for them to be repaid in the future.

The analytical model presented in this chapter is an extension of the work done by Kenneth Froot, D. Scharfstein, and J. Stein (1988), Krugman (1988a), K. Froot (1989), and S. Claessens and I. Diwan (1990b) in understanding the mechanics of a growth-oriented debt reduction strategy. The problem of incentive to invest in the presence of a large debt overhang and the need to reach a negotiated settlement of a country's Debt Problem with the need for a "package" of options (new money, buy back, and rescheduling) are specifically incorporated into the analysis.

THE MODEL

The theoretical analysis of the international debt situation presented in this chapter, proceeds in two stages. First, a simple two-period welfare maximization model is formulated, in which it is shown that an optimum amount of investment can be determined once a certain amount of debt relief and "new money" is given by the banks to a country, such that it maximizes its intertemporal utility function in the presence of a debt overhang. A "package" of options could contain several of the market-based menu of options.[5]

So, for each level of debt relief, there would exist an optimal level of investment, which maximizes the debtor country's social welfare function. In this section of the study, a framework for comparing concessional rescheduling of the existing debt with a buyback is provided. The buyback option is used here to represent the market-based options of debt reduction. Michael Dooley (1988a), Stijn Claessens (1990), and Clark (1990) have shown that the equivalency of asset exchanges could be examined by estimating their "buyback-equivalent price." Therefore, by comparing the buyback with a conventional rescheduling, there would not be any significant loss of generality of the conclusions of the model if other market-based options were also evaluated.

In the presence of a debt overhang, the debtor may maximize his or her intertemporal utility by investing nothing if the amount of debt relief granted by banks is not large enough to reduce the stock of the country's debt below a threshold level to put it on the right side of the Debt-Laffer Curve.

The next stage of the theoretical analysis provided in this study, accounts for the fact that for banks to grant a country a certain amount of debt relief, it is not possible simply to write it off from their books. Given the diverse interests of the different banks in different countries, it would be in the interest of the debtor to go for a negotiated settlement of its Debt Problem wherein a "package" of the market-based menu of options would be included. In the context of the most recent debt and debt service reduction (DDSR) agreement between Mexico and its commercial bank creditors, van Wijnbergen has stated:

To maximize the amount of debt relief, there is no doubt that Mexico had to offer its creditors a menu of choices. The reason why a single-option deal would have reduced the amount of debt relief lies in the differences in regulatory and tax environment that Mexico's various commercial creditors face. For this reason, different schemes that would present equal debt relief to Mexico, could imply very different costs to its creditors. Thus restricting the choice to one instrument only would, for given willingness to grant relief by creditors, unambiguously reduce the amount of relief actually received by Mexico. [van Wijnbergen (1990), p. 11]

Suppose there is an economy that faces a large inherited stock of debt D_0 in period 0, which it has to pay back to external creditors with interest at period 2. This formulation is similar to those discussed by Froot, Scharfstein, and Stein (1988), Krugman (1988a), Froot (1989), and Claessens and Diwan (1990b). In period 0, the debtor declares that it is having a debt-servicing problem and initiates discussions with its external creditors to negotiate a package involving debt and debt service reduction (DDSR) options. In period 1, it pays x_1 to its external creditors which is less than what it was supposed to pay on the basis of its original contractual payments (say rD_o, assuming no amortization payments were due in period 1).

In period 1, creditors agree to grant the country new loans (NM) and debt relief (x). Assume the debtor country borrows $NM = (rD_o - x_1)$ in period 1, that is, the new money from its creditors to pay for its debt service shortfall in period 1, while negotiations with its external creditors are in progress about the terms of the DDSR package for the entire debt, which will fall due in period 2. This assumption is plausible given that, as Krugman has stated, in the presence of a debt overhang: "lending that would be unprofitable viewed in isolation is worth doing as a way of defending the value of existing debt" [Krugman (1989), p. 258].

Let E denote the endowment of the debtor country after making its payments to creditors in period 1, although not including the new money.

At period 1, assume that the central planner of the debtor country is maximizing a linear intertemporal utility function of the form:

$$W = U_1(C_1) + \beta C_2 \qquad (1)$$

specification for C_2 (PV of future consumption) allows for the possibility of corner solutions in the presence of a debt overhang. $U(C_1)$ is assumed to satisfy the standard concavity conditions so that U' > 0 and U" < 0. This implies that it is increasingly costly in terms of utility for the central planner in the debtor country to reduce current consumption. ß represents the country's subjective discount factor, which, because of the relative scarcity of external credit in the debtor country, would be lower than the world's discount factor.[6] The linear specification of the welfare function has been chosen for analytical simplicity. In the same spirit as Froot (1989), we assume concavity in period 1 utility so as to explore the implications of finite intertemporal substitutability without the restriction on preferences to being risk averse.[7]

The welfare maximizing level of investment, which the central planner chooses in period 1, produces an output $y = f(I)$ in period 2. Assume $f'(I) > 0$ and $f''(I) < 0$, implying decreasing returns to scale in production. It is this output that is used to pay creditors in period 2.

This model, as in Froot (1989), Krugman (1989), and Claessens and Diwan (1990), begins by assuming a "gunboat mechanism," whereby external creditors would have first claim on all output that was produced from the previous period's investment to the extent that they were fully paid. The results would also hold if, instead, we assumed that creditors could impose penalties on the debtor in proportion to the value of output, although they may not be able to confiscate the entire output physically. Nevertheless, the "gunboat" assumption provides the strongest illustration of the disincentive effect of a debt overhang on investment decisions in the debtor country. This extreme assumption will be relaxed later, and its implications on the conclusions of the model will be examined. Let α denote the proportion of future output that creditors are able to expropriate from the debtor country in case it cannot fully meet its scheduled debt service obligations. This amount may be expropriated either through some formal agreement between the two parties or via penalties, increased fees, and margins on trade lines and other new loans.

In addition to providing new money in period 1, it is assumed that the debtor country has also negotiated some debt relief on its existing stock of "old" debt. As Dooley (1988a) has suggested, this would be beneficial for the country's existing creditors if the country is on the wrong side of the Debt-Laffer Curve (i.e., creditors would increase their revenues by granting some debt relief, x, to the country).

Case 1: $\alpha = 1$ *(i.e., all future output is expropriated by creditors in the event of non payment by the debtor).*

Under these circumstances, the country's stock of debt outstanding in period 2 would be $D = (D_o + NM - x)$ and, therefore in the next period (period 2), the creditors can expect to be paid:

$$P = \text{Min } [(D_o + NM - x)(1 + r), y] \qquad (2)$$

where r is the rate of interest charged by the creditors on the entire stock of debt. Thus, the country's consumption in period 2 is given by:

$$\text{Max } \{0, [y - (D + NM - x)(1 + r)]\} \qquad (3)$$

Therefore, the central planner in the debtor country would endeavor to find an optimal investment level, I^*, so as to maximize its social welfare function, given the amount of debt relief (x) and new money (NM), which creditors have granted to the country in period 1. Hence, the maximization problem the policy maker faces is:
Maximize

$$W^* = \text{Max } U_1(E + NM - I) + \beta \text{Max}\{0,[y - (D_o - x + NM)(1 + r)]\} \qquad (4)$$

First order condition is $dW/dI = 0$.

Differentiation of the objective function with respect to investment (I) yields:

$$- U_1 + \beta f'(I) = 0$$

or $\qquad\qquad\qquad f'(I^*) = (U_1'/\beta) \qquad (5)$

The second order condition for the maximization problem is $(d^2W/dI^2) < 0$.

Differentiation of (5) with respect to investment (I) yields:

$$- U_1'' + \beta f''(I) < 0 \qquad (6)$$

Since $U_1'' < 0$ and $f''(I) < 0$, we assume that $f(I)$ is sufficiently concave to make the second order condition hold, and an optimal level of investment I^* would exist.

The critical level of output at which all outstanding obligations would be paid off in period 2 can be denoted by:

$$f(I^c) = (D_o - x + NM)(1 + r) \qquad (7)$$

Hence, it has been shown that given an exogenously determined amount of debt relief and new money, there exists an optimal level of investment at which the debtor maximizes its welfare in the presence of a debt overhang. That is:

$$I^* = I^*(x) \text{ if } I^* > I^c$$

or $\qquad I^* = 0 \text{ if } I^* \leq I^c$ $\qquad\qquad\qquad$ (8)

Case 2: $\alpha < 1$ and Exogenous

Under these circumstances, in period 2 the creditors can be expected to receive a payment of:

$$P = \text{Min}[(D_0 + NM - x)(1 + r), \alpha y] \qquad\qquad (9)$$

where $y = f(I)$.

Therefore, the country's consumption in period 2 will be:

$$C_2 = \text{Max}\{(1 - \alpha)y, [y - (D_0 + NM - x)(1 + r)]\} \qquad (10)$$

and the optimization problem for the policy maker in the debtor country is to maximize:

$$W^* = \text{Max } U_1(E + NM - I) + \beta \text{Max}\{(1 - \alpha)y, [y - (D_0 + NM - x)(1+r)] \qquad (11)$$

The first order condition is $dW/dI = 0$. Differentiation of the objective function with respect to investment (I) yields:

$$- U_1' + \beta(1 - \alpha)f'(I) = 0 \text{ when } I^* \leq I^c \qquad\qquad (12)$$

$$- U_1' + \beta f'(I) = 0 \text{ when } I^* > I^c \qquad\qquad (13)$$

where I^c is the critical level of investment in period 1, which will result in enough output so that all outstanding obligations to external creditors will be paid off by the debtor country in period 2 (i.e., as shown in equation [7]). Hence,

$$f'(I^*) = U_1'/\beta(1 - \alpha) \text{ when } I^* \leq I^c \qquad\qquad (14)$$

and

$$f'(I^*) = U_1'/\beta \qquad \text{ when } I^* > I^c \qquad\qquad (15)$$

The second order condition for the maximization problem is $d^2W/dI^2 < 0$. Differentiation of equations (12) and (13) with respect to investment (I) yields:

$$- U_1" + \beta(1 - \alpha)f"(I) < 0 \qquad \text{for } I^* \leq I^c \qquad (16)$$

and

$$- U_1" + \beta f"(I) < 0 \qquad \text{for } I^* > I^c \qquad (17)$$

Assume that f(I) is sufficiently concave to make the second order conditions hold and for an optimal level of investment to exist. Chart 4.1 illustrates the equilibrium situation when $I^* \leq I^c$, and Chart 4.2 the situation where $I^* > I^c$.

Case 3: $\alpha < 1$ and Endogenous

In reality, the proportion of output that can be expropriated from the debtor country if it fails to make payments in full on its outstanding external debt obligations will vary from creditor to creditor. Foreign banks that have a larger exposure and/or subsidiaries in the debtor country may obtain a larger share of the country's output than other creditor banks. The analysis becomes complex at this stage, when α is itself dependent on the stock of debt owed to each external creditor. Under these circumstances, the actual amount of future output expropriated by the banks when $I^* \leq I^c$ will be somewhere *within* the shaded area in Chart 4.3. However, when $I^* > I^c$, the equilibrium condition remains unchanged. On the basis of these assumptions, when the country does not make contractual payments on its external debt under a debt overhang situation, the total proportion of output (α) expropriated by banks will be the sum of the proportion extracted by each bank (α_i). This, in turn, would depend on the debt owed by the country to each creditor bank (d_i), among other factors. That is,

$$\alpha_i = f(d_i), \quad f' > 0$$

where d_i is the debt owed to that ith. bank and

$$\alpha = \sum_{i=1}^{n} \alpha_i$$

Hence, $\alpha = f(d_i)$.

In addition to the aforementioned considerations, if one also incorporates the fact that the amount of "new money" (nm_i) and debt relief

(x_i) that is granted by each bank will also depend on its exposure in the

Chart 4.1
Equilibrium Situation with Exogenous Alpha - Case 1

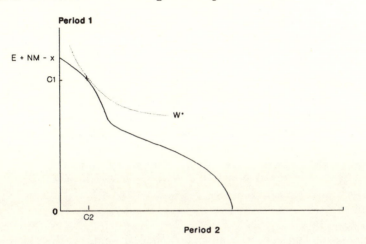

Chart 4.2
Equilibrium Situation with Exogenous Alpha - Case 2

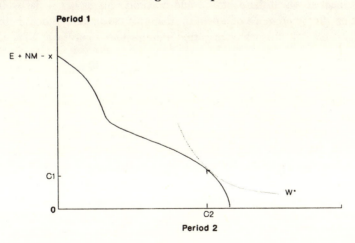

Chart 4.3
Equilibrium Situation with Endogenous Alpha - Case 3

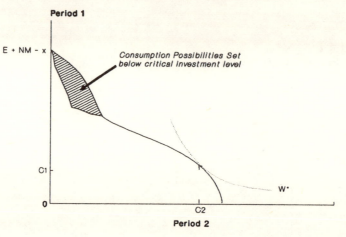

debtor country under consideration, the complexity of the analysis increases further.

Nevertheless, the analysis provided clearly shows that for each level of debt relief granted by the banks, there would be an optimal level of investment at which the debtor would maximize his or her social welfare function. In the presence of a debt overhang, if the amount of debt relief is not large enough, the debtor may find it optimal not to invest at all (i.e., $I^* = 0$).

This is a crucial result, because the amount of debt relief that would be provided by external creditors will depend on several factors, such as tax, regulatory, and accounting factors in the creditors' countries, long-term business interests of the banks in the geographical region and, last but not the least, the price (often the secondary market price for the country's debt) at which old debt is exchanged for new debt instruments, such as exit bonds. It is this issue that we now address in the following section of this study.

ECONOMIC FEASIBILITY OF A BUYBACK OPERATION

In this section, the costs and benefits of a buyback operation are evaluated analytically, and the results compared with those of a standard exercise of rescheduling the country's debt. The analysis does not look at other options of the market-based menu because, for each option (such as exit bonds), it is possible to find a buyback equivalent price, so that the material costs and benefits would be the same as a buyback operation that was carried out at the buyback-equivalent price of the instrument.[8] In addition to the *price* at which the buyback operation is carried out (e.g., the secondary market price for the debtor country's debt), the *source* of the funds which are used for the buyback (own reserves, grants, or concessional loans from official agencies, such as the International Monetary Fund or the World Bank) is also crucial in determining the economic feasibility of achieving a desired amount of reduction of existing debt obligations of a country.[9] The model that is presented here explicitly takes this factor into account. The extent to which resources available for a buyback are non-additional, that is , they come out of previously earmarked aid and project lending budgets of donors, there will be an opportunity cost associated with them. There will be some foregone income that could have been generated had those funds been used for productive investment within the economy. Obviously, the use of the debtor country's own resources (e.g., international reserve assets) for the debt reduction operation will have an opportunity cost associated with it. The measure used to compare the buyback of eligible debt using a specified amount of funds with other options is the *Net Present Value of Debt Service Relief.*

Let D_t denote the country's external debt outstanding in period 1, which is being considered for the debt buyback operation. For simplicity, we assume that the original scheduled debt service payments call for no amortization payments for the foreseeable future.[10] Hence, at any point in time, the interest payment (i_t) owed to commercial banks is:

$$i_t = D_o(L_t + S_1) \tag{18}$$

where $1 \leq t \leq T$.

T is the terminal year of the projection period over which the net present value measure would be calculated when comparing the buyback option with other market-based debt reduction options. As in the Mexican case, where the commercial bank claims were variable rate loans charging a spread over the six-month U.S.$ London Interbank Offer Rate (LIBOR),

S_1 is assumed to be the spread over LIBOR charged on the outstanding external debt prior to any debt renegotiation.[11] D_0 is the existing stock of debt in period 0 before debt restructuring. L_t is the LIBOR at time t. Under these simplifying assumptions, the present value of the future stream of debt service payments *before* the debt buyback is:

$$PV_1 = \sum_{t=1}^{T} \frac{D_0(L_t + S_t)}{(1+r)^t}$$

where *r* is the rate of discount at which the future payments are discounted. It should be noted that the debt country, as a result of external credit constraints, will have a higher discount rate than the representative world interest rate.

It is implicitly being assumed that the debtor country is willing to service the debt that will be left over after the debt reduction operation is completed. The prebuyback debt service is crucial in arriving at the value of the debt service relief from debt restructuring. Although this is not the case for Mexico, there may be cases where a country has not paid its bank creditors for a long time and is accumulating arrears. So when they pay anything to these creditors after debt renegotiation (after some debt reduction, *x*, were granted by their creditors), their debt service relief will in fact be *negative*. However, it should be kept in mind that, whenever the debtor country would open negotiations with its external creditors in order to arrive at a negotiated settlement of its Debt Problem, the creditors would begin discussions with the scheduled debt service obligations as the benchmark, and then add moratorium interest for the entire period over which a country had not paid its scheduled obligations to arrive at the amount of debt outstanding that is to be renegotiated. This has, indeed, been the case for several low-income countries in Africa that are seeking to benefit from debt reduction.

As regards financing the buyback operation, in cases where a country has signed a formal agreement with commercial banks, there may be legal impediments to using the debtor country's own resources for a buyback operation (e.g., *pari passu* and sharing clauses) unless *all* participating banks consented to this endeavor. This may be a highly time-consuming task. The presence of a Steering Committee consisting of the country's major commercial bank creditors (as in the case of Mexico) makes this task somewhat easier. Nevertheless, given the different motivations and interests of each group of bank creditors, a debt reduction package consisting of simply a buyback of existing debt at a discount (probably that quoted in the secondary market for LDC debt) is extremely unlikely, hence the need for a package of options that, in the end, would allow the country to reduce its debt by the agreed amount (x).

In the theoretical framework being discussed here, it is assumed initially that all the funds that are available for the buyback have been obtained in the form of grants from official sources. Then, the model is extended to include the possibility of obtaining concessional loans from official sources (e.g., funds from the World Bank and IMF under the auspices of the Brady Initiative, as has been the case in Mexico, the Philippines, and Costa Rica).

For the debtor country, only those funds that are nonadditional (i.e., that would have been provided by donors anyway for other purposes, such as project financing) will have an opportunity cost associated with them. Any additional funds obtained from donors for the buyback would make it more attractive for the country to proceed with the buyback. It is assumed here that all the donor financing that is provided for the buyback is nonadditional.[12]

Buyback Financed by Grants

Let official sources provide B amount of resources at time t = 1 for a one-time buyback of existing eligible external debt at a "negotiated" price, p. The buyback price, which is negotiated between the debtor and its creditors, could be at or about the secondary market price for the country's debt. If a price is not "negotiated" up front, the debtor country will incur a loss if the secondary market price begins to rise once the possibility of a country buying back its debt is filtered on to the market.[13]

Then the amount of debt outstanding after the one-time buyback is:

$$D_t - \frac{B}{p}$$

Now suppose that the remaining debt (which is not repurchased) is rescheduled at a spread of S_2 over LIBOR with $S_1 > S_2$. Therefore, the debt service due each year *after* negotiating this DDSR package is given by:

$$DS_t = [D_o - (B/p)](L_t + S_2), \quad t = 1, \ldots, T \tag{19}$$

We continue to assume that no amortization payments are due during t = 1,

T so that the stock of debt will be $[D_1 - (B/p)]$ after the debt renegotiation. The debt service *relief* each year will be given by:

$$DSR_t = D_o(S_1 - S_2) + (B/p)(L_t + S_2) \tag{20}$$

The above equation shows that the debt service relief each year will consist of two components:

- The debt service relief resulting from the rescheduling at the lower spread (S_2) over LIBOR;
- The debt service relief resulting from the one-time buyback of existing debt.

It can be gleaned from equation (20) that *the lower the buyback price and more favorable the terms of rescheduling are (in terms of a lower spread S_2), the higher the debt service relief for any particular year will be.* In addition, the debt service relief from a buyback operation will be substantially reduced if the spread over LIBOR after rescheduling (S_2) is very low (making the second term of equation [11] small). In fact, *if S_2 is low enough, the buyback option may not be attractive from the point of view of debt service reduction, and a simple rescheduling under the favorable terms is preferable.*

Hence, at the time period 0, the present value of the future stream of debt service relief (in period 1 to T) from a buyback operation carried out in period 1 is given by:

$$PV(DSR) = \sum_{t=1}^{T} \frac{DSR_t}{(1+r)^t} \tag{21}$$

Substituting equation (20) in (21), we arrive at:

$$PV(DSR) = \sum_{t=1}^{T} \frac{D_0(S_1 - S_2) + (B/p)(L_t + S_2)}{(1+r)^t} \tag{22}$$

with $0 < r < 1$, r being the rate of time preference of the debtor country. In the model formulated here, r is exogenous (whose value will depend on the relative scarcity of capital and foreign exchange in the debtor country if the debtor is evaluating the DDSR package, and the rate of time preference for the individual bank, if it is evaluating the DDSR package).

From equation (22), a reduced form expression for the present value of debt service relief can be derived:

$$
\overset{+\;\;+\quad\quad ?\quad +\;+\;\;-\;\;-}{PV(DSR) = f(D_o,(S_1 - S_2),\ S_2,\ B,\ L_t,\ p,\ r)} \tag{23}
$$

The sign above each variable in the expression denotes the sign of the partial derivative of the present value function with respect to that particular factor. From equation (23), it can be gleaned that except for S_2, the signs of the partial derivatives with respect to the other factors in the expression are unambiguous. The ambiguity in the net effect of S_2 on the present value of debt service relief is the result of the nature of its relationship with the other factors in the expression (such as the amount of debt left over after the buyback and the buyback price).

Equation (22) can also be used to derive *the effect of a change in the buyback price (p) on the present value of debt service relief* (our measure of the attractiveness of the debt reduction option to the debtor country), *ceteris paribus*.

Let a unit increase in the buyback price be denoted by an increase from p_1 cents per dollar of debt to p_2 cents per dollar. Then from equation (22) the change in the present value of debt service relief from the buyback operation is given by:

$$\underline{\Lambda}PV = PV(DSR) \text{ at } p_2 - PV(DSR) \text{ at } p_1$$

which can be written as:

$$\Delta PV = \sum_{t=1}^{T} (B/p_2)(L_t + S_2) - \sum_{t=1}^{T} (B/p_1)(L_t + S_t)$$

or

$$\Delta PV = B[(1/p_2) - (1/p_1)] \sum_{t=1}^{T} (L_t + S_2) \tag{24}$$

Since $p_2 > p_1$, it implies that $[(1/p_2) - (1/p_1)] < 0$, so that $\underline{\Lambda} PV < 0$.

This implies that, *when the buyback price increases, the present value of debt service relief will be lower.* This result supports the conclusions of Dooley (1987) and Bulow and Rogoff (1988), and suggests that a buyback operation would provide a larger benefit to the debtor country in terms of the present value of debt service relief if a buyback price were set *prior* to the actual operation. Otherwise, an increase in the secondary market price that will follow after the possibility of a buyback is announced will lower the benefits the debtor country would receive by carrying out a DDSR operation.

Buyback Financed By Grants and Concessional Loans

Let F denote the total amount of concessional financing that is available to the debtor country for the buyback operation. Once again, assume that these resources are nonadditional and, therefore, have an associated opportunity cost. Let i_c be the fixed rate of interest at which these loans are borrowed from official creditors, and maintain the assumption of continuous rolling over of scheduled amortization payments, for simplicity.

Under these circumstances, the debt service *each year* after the buyback would be:

$$DS_t' = (D_o - B/p - F/p)(L_1 + S_2) + i_c F \qquad (25)$$

where $t = 1, ..., T$. Obviously, the debtor country would pay a higher debt service DS_t' each year when it has borrowed for the buyback operation rather than just relying on loans (so that the debt service each year would have been DS_t, which was discussed in the previous section). Now, the stock of debt after the buyback will be:

$$(D_o - B/p - F/p)$$

and the debt service relief each year compared to scheduled debt service obligations would be:

$$DSR_t' = D_o(S_1 - S_2) + (B/p)(L_1 + S_2) + F\{[(L_1 + S_2)/p] - i_c\} \qquad (26)$$

The above expression is quite similar to the one derived for the donor financed buyback operation, except for the addition of the last term. Now, the debt service relief in each period will also depend on the amount of concessional loans available (F) for the buyback, as well as the interest rate charged on these concessional loans.

It can also be gleaned from equation (26) that when concessional loans are also used to finance a buyback operation, the debt service relief each period will increase only if the terms of the rescheduling and the buyback price are favorable enough and the interest rate on the concessional loans is low enough. Specifically, for a buyback financed by concessional loans to lead to an increase in debt service relief for the debtor country the following condition must hold:

$$(L_1 + S_2)/p > i_c \qquad (27)$$

This condition simply implies that, for concessional loans to be beneficial for the country that is embarking on a buyback operation, these loans should not be too costly relative to the debt service reduction they would generate through their use in the buyback operation.

Once again, the present value of the future stream of debt service relief (in periods 1 to T) from the buyback operation can be derived.

$$PV(DSR_v) = \sum_{t=1}^{T} \frac{D_0(S_1 - S_2) + (B/p)(L_t + S_2) + F[(L_t + S_2)/p - i_c]}{(1+r)^t}$$

where $0 < r < 1$.

The reduced form equation for PV(DSR'$_v$) is:

$$\overset{+\ \ +\ \ ?\ \ \ \ \ \ \ +\ +\ +\ -\ -\ -}{PV(DSR'_v) = f(D_o, (S_1 - S_2), S_2, B, F, L_t, p, r, i_c)} \qquad (28)$$

This present value measure may be used to compare the potential benefit of a buyback operation with that of other market-based menu options for dealing with the Debt Problem of countries that have a large debt overhang.

In the theoretical analysis presented so far in this chapter, the simplifying assumption was made that the spread charged by banks on rescheduled loans (S_2) was given exogenously. However, S_2 is often arrived at after lengthy negotiations between the debtor country and the creditor banks, that is S_2 is in fact *endogenous*. A more complete analysis would require a closer investigation of the choice mechanism through which each bank chooses a market-based instrument of debt reduction for the debtor country under consideration. The final outcome of which option (or combination of options) a creditor bank would choose depends on several factors, such as the status of negotiations between the two parties; its exposure in that country; its perception of the future repayment capacity of the debtor country; the tax, accounting, and regulatory regime facing the creditor bank; its long-term business strategy in the country; and the precedence that would be set once the bank chose an option. In this sense, if the bank agrees to reschedule the debt owed to it by Mexico, the terms of the rescheduling (S_2) would, in fact, be influenced by the aforementioned factors. A more detailed analysis of the factors that make S_2 endogenous is beyond the scope of this study.

CONCLUSIONS

In this chapter, an analytical framework was provided to show that in the presence of a debt overhang, it would be possible for a country to have the incentive to invest for future consumption and debt service given that it could negotiate a debt and debt service reduction "package" consisting of new money (to pay for the shortfall in its debt service payments in period 1) and a reduction in the stock of existing debt (by an amount x). This model can be used to illustrate the Debt-Laffer Curve hypothesis, that is, for countries that have a very large stock of external debt outstanding, by granting some debt relief now, creditors can increase their revenues in the future, after the debtor country reaps the benefits from its investment and growth, and is successful in its economic adjustment program.

The adoption of a "package" of options to deal with a country's Debt Problem is in conformity with the fact that different creditors have different motivations and will not accept to simply writing down their claims on a country. Tax, accounting, regulatory, considerations and the long-term business interests of banks determine their strategy in dealing with a country's debt obligations to them.

In this light, the next stage in this analytical framework is to examine some of the factors that will influence the ultimate mix of options banks may grant a country as a way of providing it debt relief. The benefit to the debtor country is evaluated in terms of the present value of debt service relief of a buyback under alternative financing techniques. On the basis of this framework for analysis of a buyback operation, it can be concluded that:

- A buyback operation may *not* always be the best option to adopt in terms of the present value of debt service relief to the country concerned. If the terms of the rescheduling are favorable enough, the buyback option would give a lower present value of debt service relief. Under these circumstances, rescheduling of the existing debt may be a more attractive option on the basis of the present value criteria.[14]

- The lower the buyback price, the higher the debt service relief for any particular year will be. Hence, on the basis of the present value model developed in this model, the debtor country may prefer to buy back its external debt outstanding in order to reduce its future debt service burden when the secondary market price for its debt is very low.[15]

- If concessional loans are available to a country for the buyback operation, it is *not* always the best use of these resources. Using concessional loans for a buyback operation will be beneficial to the country if, and only if, the buyback price is low enough and the interest rate on these concessional loans is low enough.

NOTES

1. See Willem Buiter (1985), Rudger Dornbusch (1977), Ritu Anand and Sweder van Wijnbergen (1989), Drazen, J. and Helpman, E., (1987) and Vito Tanzi (1986) for excellent insights on this issue.

2. See Eichengreen and Lindert (1989) for an excellent historical review of the costs of default.

3. See Brun and Gooptu (1990) for details on the role and cost of short-term trade credit to LDCs.

4. See Sudarshan Gooptu (1989), Johnathan Hay and Michel Bouchet (1989b), and Krugman (1988, 1989) for details on the factors that influence the choice of options of banks in a debtor country's DDSR package.

5. See Froot (1989) for a theoretical analysis of the welfare costs and benefits of each group of market-based options.

6. If r is the representative world interest rate, then the world discount factor is $1/(1 + r)$. Assuming $r = 0$, the world discount factor equals 1 so $\beta < 1$.

7. A strictly linear welfare function would imply that the elasticity of intertemporal substitutability is infinite. See Elhanan Helpman (1987) for a discussion of the risk-sharing issues of nonlinear intertemporal utility functions in this context.

8. See Clark (1990), and Claessens, et. al. (1990) for discussions of the methodology for evaluating the equivalency of different debt instruments and options in a DDSR operation.

9. See Gooptu (1989b) "The Market-based Menu Approach in Sub-Saharan Africa," *World Bank CFS Informal Financial Notes Series*, No. 11, for a detailed discussion of the factors that should be taken into account when formulating a debt reduction operation.

10. This is, indeed, a valid assumption in cases where the debtor country is successful in rolling over its scheduled amortization payments continuously after negotiations with its external creditors. Conclusions of the model would not change significantly if the possibility of positive amortization payments were incorporated into the analysis.

11. Minor modifications could be made to this model to allow for fixed interest rate debt. Specifically, L_t could be taken as zero and S_1 to be the fixed rate of interest charged on these loans.

12. The conclusions of the model will not change if only a part of the donor financing is nonadditional in nature.

13. See Bulow and Rogoff (1988) for a discussion of why the secondary market price of a country's debt would tend to rise after its stock of debt becomes smaller after a debt reduction operation.

14. This conclusion reinforces van Wijnbergen's contention that "debt relief offers the most certain way to reduce future net transfers for a country for a long time to come. However, new money commitments if credible and stretched out far enough into the future, could have served equally well" [van Wijnbergen (1990), p. 7].

15. This model has been extended to include the possibility of a "staggered buyback" in Gooptu (1989a), "Analysis of Buyback Options in Sub-Saharan Africa," *World Bank, CFS Informal Financial Notes Series*, No. 12, December 1989.

5

Empirical Findings
from the Mexican Case

DOES THE LEVEL OF DEBT MATTER?

In view of the discussion on the Mexican economy that was provided in Chapters 2 and 3 of this study and the analytical framework that was provided in Chapter 4 to evaluate the welfare maximizing behavior of the debtor who is faced with a large debt overhang, the task at hand is to focus our attention on domestic investment in Mexico. Our objective is to try to ascertain whether the level of external debt outstanding and disbursed does, indeed, create an impediment towards increased investment and, in turn, future growth in Mexico. In other words, the question being addressed is whether there is currently any available evidence on the existence of a debt overhang in Mexico.[1]

If a situation of a debt overhang exists, it would imply that the stock of external debt is large enough so that private economic agents would face a disincentive to invest in Mexico, because they would expect part of their returns from their initial investment to be taxed in some way (inflation tax, domestic debt, among others) by the Government in order to pay external creditors. Thus, one would observe a sustained decline in investment levels within the country as the stock of debt surpasses a threshold level beyond which private individuals within the country consider the debt overhang to be a reality.

Although there has been some progress in developing theoretical models in evaluating the debt overhang situation in the recent past (as discussed in the previous chapter), very little empirical work has been done on this subject.   There may be two possible reasons for this: (1) the task of identifying the exact level of external debt outstanding beyond which the "disincentive effect" of a debt overhang kicks in is an extremely difficult one, and (2) domestic investment may be falling in a country as a result of a deterioration in the domestic economic conditions or adverse external shocks, instead of merely an increase in the stock of external debt.

To determine whether a reduction in the stock of debt will actually lead to a sustained increase in investment levels, because of an alleviation of the debt overhang, one needs data on several time periods. Given the fact that debt reduction has only become possible in the last two years or so (with the Mexican Aztec Bonds and the 1988-89 Brady-type debt restructuring between Mexico and its commercial bank creditors), we do not have enough ex-post information to draw concrete results on this matter. Nevertheless, in an endeavor to find *some* indication of the specific influence of the stock of external debt on gross domestic capital formation, we have examined the Mexican situation for the period of time over which a consistent set of data on relevant variables was available. However, results obtained should be interpreted with caution. For example, even if the results were to show that private investment increases when debt reduction takes place, it may very well be that private investment was low before because of the scarcity of investible resources in the private sector (even if private firms wanted to invest).   Debt reduction would be one way of making more resources available to the private sector for productive investment.   When public sector debt is extinguished via a debt reduction operation, it may not always be translated into an increase in available resources for private sector investment.   In addition, even if more resources were available to the private sector (via direct subsidies or through the domestic financial system), if the expectations of the private investors on the future course of the economy are not favorable, no increase in investment may be observed.

The results will also be crucially dependent on the sources of funds that are available to the private sector, at any point in time, for productive investment in the debtor country in question. If, as in the case of Mexico, revenues from oil exports form a significant part of its foreign earnings (until recently), the negative effect of a sharp decline in the price of oil in the international market may offset the positive effect of debt reduction on available resources for private sector investment.

From the discussion on the developments in Mexico during the last four decades that was provided in Chapters 2 and 3 of this study, some evidence of the negative incentive effect of a debt overhang can be gleaned. Charts 5.1 and 5.2 clearly show a sharp decline in private, public, and total gross fixed domestic investment (as a percent of GDP) in Mexico after 1982.

Chart 5.1
Public and Private Gross Domestic Fixed Capital (as a percent of GDP)

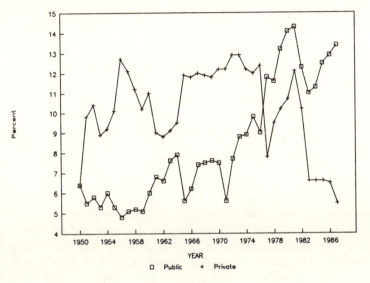

Chart 5.2
Total Gross Domestic Fixed Capital (as a percent of GDP)

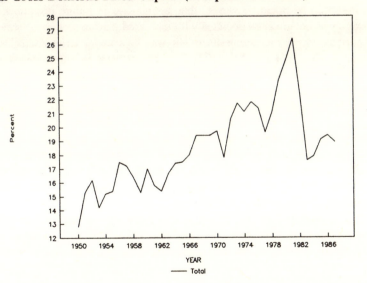

The share of private gross domestic fixed capital formation in GDP increased from 6.4 percent in 1950 to 12.1 percent in 1981 and then declined to 5.5 percent by 1987. The share of total gross domestic fixed capital formation in GDP increased from 12.8 percent in 1950 to 26.4 percent in 1981 and then declined to 18.9 percent by 1987. There was a sharp increase in Mexico's external public and publicly guaranteed debt from $33.8 billion in 1980 to $53 billion in 1981 to $81.5 billion by 1987. Mexico's total external indebtedness had jumped from $57.4 billion in 1980 to $78.2 billion in 1982 and had reached about $108 billion by 1987. At the end of 1989, Mexico owed its external creditors $102 billion, of which more than 3/4 was owed to private creditors abroad (commercial banks and suppliers).

Another result that can be gleaned from our casual empiricism (from Charts 5.1 and 5.2) is the striking similarly in the paths of private and public gross domestic fixed capital formation in Mexico during most of the period under examination (1973-89), especially during 1976 to 1982. Increases in public investment have often led to increases in private investment. This may be rationalized on the grounds that an increase in public investment in the federal government and parastatal enterprises had created an increase in demand for goods produced in the private sector; for example, public investment in the transportation and petroleum sector resulted in increased investment by firms in the spare parts and secondary petrochemical industries. In other words, some private sector investment has resulted from the backward and forward linkages of increased investment in the Mexican public sector.

It should be noted, however, that an increase in public investment in Mexico was not always associated with increased private sector investment. In periods where total domestic credit was kept under strict control as a matter of government policy (1971-76), any increase in public investment led to a crowding out of private investment in the economy. After 1976, when foreign loans were easily obtained by Mexico, both public and private sector investments were able to increase simultaneously. This relationship between public and private investments exists even in the absence of a large stock of external debt. As the stock of debt increases, initially it may lead to increases in both public and private investment expenditures simply because more resources are available in the economy. The negative incentive effect of the debt overhang will occur when the level of debt outstanding has reached a critical level.

If it is assumed that the critical level of debt at which private investors perceived Mexico to have a debt overhang was the stock of external debt outstanding in 1982, one would have observed a fall in private investment (as a share of GDP) even if foreign loans were available to private investors in Mexico. The fact of the matter is, however, that after the 1982 moratorium, voluntary lending from international financial markets to Mexico was *not* available. Therefore, the decline in private investment (and total investment for that matter) was partly the result of the scarcity of available credit, coupled with the deterioration in domestic conditions that had occurred at that time. The effect of the debt overhang does, nevertheless, contribute to the decline in private investment, especially after a few years in which stringent macroeconomic adjustment measures were implemented and no significant economic growth was observed. Between 1983-89, this had indeed been the case in Mexico, where the real rate of growth in GDP in 1988 (1.3 percent) was much below the average real rate of growth of GDP for 1950-70 (about 6 percent per annum), even after stringent adjustment measures were implemented between 1983-88. However, a decline in Mexico's foreign exchange earnings resulting from the falling oil prices also contributed to the general lack of available resources for both private and public sector investments during the period.

Our evaluation of the Mexican situation has shown that policy actions and adverse external shocks have often led to increases in real interest rates in Mexico, which, in turn, were responsible for the observed decline in private investment even in periods where the external debt to GDP ratio was sustainable by the Mexican current account balance and domestic resources. Isolating the negative "incentive effect" on private investment resulting from the debt overhang from the standard "interest rate effect" is a difficult task. Given that the existence of a debt overhang gives rise to expectations on the part of private investors about *future* events, this task is all the more complex.

PRELIMINARY ECONOMETRIC ANALYSIS

For reasons mentioned in the previous section of this chapter, there are several factors that could explain the behavior of private investment in a country. In the case of a developing country like Mexico, an analysis of all these factors becomes difficult because of the lack of a consistent and complete time series for several of these variables (e.g., average cost of investable funds in Mexico, unit labor costs, and the marginal productivity of capital, among others). The econometric analysis provided in this study is only a first step towards a more complete analysis of private investment in Mexico. Our focus is on the effect of Mexico's external debt burden, if any, on private domestic investment levels in Mexico. In an endeavor to determine the effect of the country's stock of debt outstanding and disbursed on the level of private gross fixed capital formation, alternative regressions models were specified and estimated using the ordinary least squares (OLS) method for Mexican data for the period 1950-87 (i.e. thirty-eight observations were fitted). The influence of omitted variables would be embodied in the error term. A summary of the regression results is presented in Table 5.1. A list of variables, the data used for these preliminary regressions, and details of the econometric analysis are provided in Appendices D and E.

A regression with the share of private gross domestic fixed capital formation in gross domestic product (RPVTGDFI) as the dependent variable, and the share of public gross fixed capital formation in GDP (RPUBGDFI) and Mexico's public and publicly guaranteed debt outstanding and disbursed (PPGDODUS) as explanatory variables was estimated. The coefficient of the debt stock variable (PPGDODUS) was negative and significant at even a 1 percent level of significance. The constant term, embodying the systematic component of factors not included in the model, was statistically significant at the 1 percent level of significance. The coefficient of the public investment explanatory variable (RPUBGDFI) had a positive sign and was statistically significant at the 10 percent level of significance, but not at the 5 percent level. The F-test for the overall model gave a p-value of 0.0002, implying that the model was correctly specified. The Durbin-Watson (DW) statistic was low. The null hypothesis of no serial correlation of the error term was rejected at the 5 percent level of significance, since DW = 0.9, which was less than the lower bound of the critical values $d_l = 1.37$ (for n = 38 and k = 2), thereby implying that positive serial correlation of the error terms was a problem in the estimated regression model.

The results of the DW test show that the error terms of consecutive years were positively correlated. This may be because of correlation in the measurement error component of the error term or, more likely, because of the correlation over time, which may be present in the cumulative effects of omitted variables.[2]   OLS coefficient estimates will be unbiased and consistent, but not efficient. When the error terms exhibit positive serial correlation, the standard error of the coefficient estimates of the OLS regression will be smaller than the true standard errors (i.e., the standard error of the regression will be biased downward).   Under these circumstances, parameter estimates will appear to be more precise than they really are. Hence, there will be a tendency to reject the null hypothesis that the true coefficient of the independent variable in the regression equation is zero when, in fact, it should not be rejected.

Table 5.1
Results of the Preliminary Regressions

Dependent Variable	Constant	Independent Variables			R Square (adjusted)	DW	p-value for full model
		RPUBGDFI	PRGDODUS	TODODRS			
		Coefficient Estimates					
RPVTGDFI	9.01	0.30	-0.076		0.36	0.90	0.0002
	(7.50)	(1.74)	(-3.87)				
RPVTGDFI	8.87	0.32		-0.056	0.35	0.86	0.0002
	(7.05)	(1.75)		(-3.73)			

Note: Numbers in brackets below coefficient estimates denote t-ratios.

Table 5.2
Autocorrelation Functions and the Q-Test

				Variable				
Lags	RPVTGDFI	RPUBGDFI	PPGDODUS	TODODDRS	DIFRPVTI	DIFRPUBI	DIFPPGD	DIFTDDRS
1	0.652	0.894	0.902	0.911	-0.013	-0.094	0.532	0.723
2	0.416	0.797	0.798	0.816	-0.157	-0.066	0.457	0.513
3	0.270	0.712	0.692	0.714	-0.067	-0.100	0.310	0.402
4	0.122	0.649	0.581	0.603	-0.086	-0.132	0.303	0.394
5	0.021	0.609	0.465	0.482	0.108	0.028	0.399	0.283
6	-0.010	0.537	0.353	0.364	0.107	0.093	0.344	0.292
7	0.019	0.415	0.246	0.248	-0.113	-0.017	0.195	0.170
8	0.050	0.294	0.180	0.162	0.034	-0.106	0.119	0.041
9	0.029	0.194	0.117	0.096	0.113	-0.028	0.030	-0.001
10	-0.088	0.117	0.059	0.038	-0.046	-0.117	-0.004	0.020
Q-Statistic	26.5	126.39	102.99	107.63	3.27	2.81	48.07	48.1
Significant at 5% level	Yes	Yes	Yes	Yes	No	No	Yes	Yes

Note: Critical value for Q at 5% level of significance is 18.31 (chi-square for k = 10)

When the stock of *total* external debt outstanding and disbursed (TODODDRS) was included as an explanatory variable instead of the stock of public and publicly guaranteed debt (PPGDODUS), the coefficient estimate was still negative and significant at the 1 percent level of significance. In this case as well, the coefficient estimate for public investment (RPUBGDFI) was statistically significant at the 10 percent level of significance (but not at the 5 percent level) and continued to have a positive sign. In this regression as well, the DW statistic was low and implied the existence of positive serial correlation in the error terms. The F-test for the overall model once again showed that the model was correctly specified.

The DW statistic tests only for first order serial correlation of the error terms, that is, when error terms for *consecutive* time periods are correlated with each other. Our preliminary econometric analysis of the Mexican data showed that there was positive serial correlation of the error terms. One approach to correct for this problem (i.e., the violation of one of the Gauss-Markov conditions that the error terms should be independent of each other) is to use the Cochrane-Orcutt Procedure, in which one estimates a regression by transforming all the variables by "generalized differencing." However, the sample estimate of the autocorrelation coefficient, which is used for the differencing, will be subject to sampling errors. An alternative approach is to estimate a *first-difference equation*, that is, the dependent variable and independent variables are differenced and then regressed. The implicit assumption being made in this case is that the first differences of the errors $(e_t - e_{t-1})$ are independent. The first difference equation is generally estimated with no constant term. Inclusion of a constant term is valid only if there is a linear trend term in the original (nondifferenced) model. When comparing equations in levels and first differences, one cannot compare the R^2's because the explained variables are different. The residual sums of squares can be compared, but only after making a rough adjustment.[3]   In this context, G. S. Maddala has stated:

Usually, with time series data, one gets high R^2 values if the regressions are estimated with the levels y_t and x_t but one gets low R^2 values if the regressions are estimated in first differences $(y_t - y_{t-1})$ and $(x_t - x_{t-1})$. Since a high R^2 is usually considered as proof of a strong relationship between the variables under investigation, there is a strong tendency to estimate the equations in levels rather than in first differences. This is sometimes called the R^2 Syndrome. However, if the DW statistic is very low, it often implies a mist equation, no matter what the value of the R^2 is. In such cases, one should estimate the regression equation in first differences and if R^2 is low, this merely indicated that the variables y and x are not related to each other. [Maddala (1988), p. 191]

Since the DW Statistic tests for first-order serial correlation only, it would be prudent first to examine the mean of the series and whether the time series need to be differenced only once before they become stationary. The problem of spurious correlations that emerges from nonstationary series is also discussed in the next section.

"STATIONARITY" AND SPURIOUS CORRELATIONS

If the time series (or "stochastic" process) under consideration is *nonstationary*, we cannot apply standard OLS regression techniques to model the relationship of different variables, because the structural relationship changes over time. If, on the other hand, the process is invariant with respect to time, that is, it is *stationary*, it is possible to formulate a meaningful model consisting of a fixed coefficient regression that can be estimated from past data.[4] Although it can be difficult to model nonstationary processes, they can often be transformed into stationary or approximately stationary processes. Specifically, many nonstationary time series have the desirable property that if they are differenced one or more times, the resulting series will be stationary (i.e., the nonstationary series are homogeneous), the order of homogeneity being the number of times the original series must be differenced before a stationary series results.

A plot of the *autocorrelation function* (ACF) of the series can help in determining whether the original series is stationary and also help in determining the appropriate number of times a homogeneous nonstationary series should be differenced to arrive at a stationary series.

The autocorrelation functions for RPVTGDFI, RPUBGDFI, PPGDODUS and TDODDRS were plotted. In all the cases, it was observed that the series would have to be differenced in order to achieve stationarity. In each case, the autocorrelation function declines gradually. Partial autocorrelation plots were also generated. These showed that first order differencing should take care of the nonstationarity problem. Q-statistics to test for the existence of white noise in each series were also performed for ten lags (k = 10). In each case, the null hypothesis that all the ACFs (for ten lags) were not significantly different from zero was rejected at the 5 percent level of significance. This further supported the need for differencing of each series.

Table 5.3
Results of Regressions with First Differences

Dependent Variable	Constant	Independent Variables DIFRPUBI	DIFPPGD	DIFTDDRS	DODDLMI	R Square (adjusted)	DW	p-value for full model
		Coefficient Estimates						
DIFRPVTI	0.27 (0.95)	-0.37 (-1.65)	0.003 (0.04)		-1.44 (-2.13)	0.096	1.88	0.098
DIFRPVTI	0.34 (1.16)	-0.35 (-1.55)		-0.0245 (-0.46)	-1.37 (-2.09)	0.10	1.88	0.089

Note: Numbers in brackets below coefficient estimates denote t-ratios.

REGRESSION OF FIRST DIFFERENCES

The first difference of each series was computed and its autocorrelation functions were plotted. Q-tests for ten lags were performed. After differencing, each series did become stationary, and only white noise remained (i.e., the Q-Test was unable to reject the null hypothesis that the autocorrelation functions for ten lags were all not significantly different from zero).

More rigorous tests that investigate whether the original series follow a random walk have been constructed, for example, the Dicky-Fuller Test for Autoregressive Time Series with a *unit root*.[5] If a test fails to reject the hypothesis of a random walk, one can difference the series in question before using it in a regression. Without differencing, the original series could be characterized as having a *random walk*. A regression of one series (before differencing) against another would then lead to spurious results. The variance of the error terms would not be finite, and the Gauss-Markov theorem would not hold. First difference regressions eliminate the trend component arising from a unit root, thereby taking care of the problem of spurious correlations. For small sample sizes, differencing may result in a loss of information about the long-run relationship between two variables. In cases where two variables follow random walks, but a linear combination of these variables is stationary, the *co-integration* procedure can be adopted in order to examine any possible structural relationship that may exist between the variables. This is beyond the scope of this study.

In this study, regression models for first differenced series were estimated, and a dummy variable to illustrate the debt overhang situation was incorporated. Results obtained are shown in Table 5.3.

After differencing the Mexican time series data for 1950-87, there were thirty-seven observations that were then regressed with the first differences of the ratio of private investment to GDP (DIFRPVTI) as the dependent variable. First differences of the ratio of public investment to GDP (DIFRPUBI) and the level of external debt (either DIFPPGD or DIFTDDRS) were included as explanatory variables in the regression.

Since not every dollar of external debt has the negative incentive effect on private investment associated with it, an appropriate proxy to represent the debt overhang situation had to be incorporated in the econometric analysis. One approach (a la Eduardo Borensztein [1990]) would be to identify a year in which the "debt overhang" problem was obvious (say 1982, when Mexico declared a moratorium on debt service payments owed to its commercial bank creditors) that is, the critical level of external obligations beyond which the negative incentive effect became relevant, and then to define a proxy variable as the difference between the level of external debt in any year and the threshold level (of 1982). However, the results of the inclusion of this proxy variable instead of the level of external debt outstanding in that year in the regression would not be any different, because this proxy variable merely changes the reference year (or origin) to 1982. If two regression equations are estimated, one with the proxy variable and the other with the level of external debt as independent variables, their coefficient estimates will be identical.

The approach used in this study was to define a dummy variable, DODDUM1, which had a value of zero prior to 1982 and unity thereafter. This was done on the assumption that the level of external debt from 1982 was above the critical level beyond which the negative incentive effect on private investment became applicable.

Regressions with a constant term were estimated for the differenced series along with the dummy variable for the debt overhang.[6] In the first model with DIFRPUBI, DIFDPPGD, and DODDUM1 as independent variables, only the coefficient of the dummy variable for the debt overhang (DODDUM1) was statistically significant at the 5 percent level of significance. R^2 was extremely low, but DW = 1.88 (showing no serial correlation since DW > d_u = 1.66 at the 5 percent level of significance). The F-test for the full model rejected the null hypothesis that the coefficients of the independent variables, taken together, were not significantly different from zero. Similar results were obtained when the first differences of total external debt (DIFTDDR5) were included in the regression instead of the first differences of public and publicly guaranteed debt (DIFPPGD). Once again, the coefficient of the dummy variable was negative and significant. The F-test for the full model rejected the null hypothesis that all the coefficients of the independent were not significantly different from zero, at the 10 percent level of significance. The fact that the constant term was not statistically significant implied that a trend component in the original series was not important.

The domestic real interest rate was included in the regressions, but was not statistically significant and was, therefore, dropped. Regressions on the differenced series with no constant term yielded the same conclusions.

The results of the regressions with first differences do not say much about the specific influence of the debt overhang on private investment in Mexico. What is clear is that from 1982 onwards, there was a negative influence on investment in Mexico. The debt overhang could be only one of the factors that may contribute to this negative influence.

As discussed previously, we are only concerned about the negative influence of the debt overhang on private investment levels. However, if the overall effect of the stock of external debt on private investment is negative, it may be because of several factors *in addition* to the debt overhang; that is, high levels of public debt may be the result of the increase in public sector deficit that is financed from abroad and via an increase in domestic debt by offering a higher domestic real interest rate. This, in turn, would have a negative effect on private fixed domestic capital formation. This negative influence may become more dominant if there is a policy of tight domestic credit, which was the case in Mexico, so that to increase public investment there would have to be a crowding out of private investment. Hence, the overall effect of external debt accumulation per se on private investment may be positive or negative depending on the strength of these other influences, in addition to the negative effect of a debt overhang, which becomes relevant only at levels of external debt that are sufficiently high.

Hence, our empirical estimates have shed some light on the debt overhang problem in Mexico after 1982, although results obtained are by no means clear. The problem of identifying an appropriate variable to represent the debt overhang persists, and the problem of isolating its influence on private gross fixed capital formation in Mexico continues to exist. The results obtained in this study are a step in the right direction, but by no means do they answer the question about whether debt reduction will, indeed, bring about an increase in private investment in Mexico. Only time and further research in the area will tell.

NOTES

1. That is, whether Mexico currently lies on the "wrong" side of the Debt-Laffer Curve.

2. See Robert Pindyck and Daniel Rubinfeld (1991), pp. 138-45 for details on the consequences of and correction for serially correlated errors.

3. See Maddala (1988) pp. 188-90 for details.

4. See Pindyck and Rubinfeld (1991) and Maddala (1988) for details on the properties of stationary and non-stationary processes.

5. See D. A. Dickey and W. A. Fuller (1981), "Likelihood Ratio Statistics for Autoregressive Time Series with a Unite Root," *Econometrica*, Vol. 49, pp. 1057-72.

6. See Appendix C for details on the regression models estimated.

APPENDIXES

Appendix A:
Review of Past Debt
Restructuring Proposals

I. Changes in the Size of the Debt Outstanding

A. **Providing new sources of financing for debtor nations.**

Formation of an Emergency Fund by the IMF/World Bank or the commercial banks themselves. Increase in the traditional lending by the IMF/World Bank. Formation of an Export Development Fund for developing country exportables.

B. **Guarantee of Commercial Bank lending.**

Formation of a new international agency that will guarantee new commercial bank lending to developing countries. The guarantee could be provided by OECD governments and the World Bank. The provision of "Credit Insurance" by the IMF and the World Bank has also been proposed.

C. **Creation of New Financial Instruments**

Futures contracts to hedge against interest rate and commodity price fluctuations. Debtor pays fixed "real" interest rate and repayment of the principal after adjusting for inflation. Use of a zero-coupon bond or the introduction of a floating rate Consol. The introduction of new instruments with different risk characteristics than those presently available.

II.   Changes in the Terms and Conditions of Existing Debt

A. **Forgiveness of Debt Outstanding**.

Comprehensive multi-year rescheduling, lower interest rates on outstanding debt, linking of debt repayment to export earnings, debt-equity swaps, and moratorium/write-off have been proposed.

B. **Creation of a Debt Facility**.

The formation of a Rediscount Facility for commercial bank loans to developing countries by Central Bank and Export Credit Agencies. Creation of a secondary market for developing country debt. Transfer of claims to the IMF/World Bank for refunding existing debt.

III.   Other Proposals

Adjustment through growth of OECD countries, fixed exchange rates, and more of what has been done in the past (i.e. rescheduling and concerted new money from existing creditor banks). Increasing supervision of lending by the IMF and Central Banks.

Appendix B:
The "Maquiladora" Sector

The purpose of this appendix is to provide a factual background on the in-bond assembly sector of Mexico. A description of the regulatory and tax environment is included. Given the ease of entry into the "maquiladora" sector and ongoing liberalization efforts on the part of the Mexican government, the growing importance of this sector as a possible target for direct foreign investment is quite apparent.

The in-bond assembly ("maquiladora") sector of Mexico has been a very important avenue for attracting direct foreign investment in the past and continues to do so even today. The maquiladora program was set up in the later 1960s in order to allow the U.S. companies to take advantage of the cheap labor and raw materials (such as diesel fuel, electrical power, and transportation costs) available in Mexico. These firms carried out assembly operations of products that were then re-exported to the United States and to other markets. These subsidiaries of U.S. corporations receive tariff exemptions on the goods assembled in Mexico.[1] Over time, European and Japanese firms have also invested in the in-bond assembly sector of Mexico, although the share of U.S.-owned firms continues to dominate. The non-U.S. firms, by setting up maquiladoras through their U.S. subsidiaries, have also been able to take advantage of U.S. tariff exemptions given to the in-bond assembly products from Mexico. The proximity of Mexico to the U.S. has provided an additional incentive to the non-U.S. corporations to invest in the maquiladora sector of Mexico.

In 1987, the maquiladoras contributed close to $1.6 billion of value added to Mexico's balance of payments. This is second only to oil in terms of the total export earnings of the country. The number of plants in the maquiladora sector has doubled since 1983 (Chart B.1). The Electrical Machinery subsector occupies the largest share of this sector in terms of both value added and employment. When combined with the electronics firms, 45 percent of value added and 48 percent of employment in the maquiladora sector are accounted for. Transport equipment (e.g., auto parts) firms account for 25 percent of total value added and 19 percent of total employment in the maquiladora sector (Chart B.2).

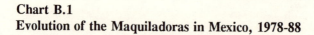

Chart B.1
Evolution of the Maquiladoras in Mexico, 1978-88

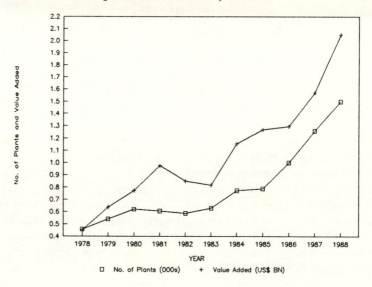

Chart B.2
Sectoral Distribution of Maquiladoras

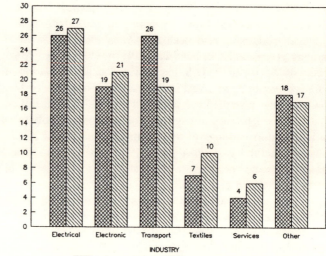

LOCATION

Eighty-two percent (82%) of existing plants in the maquiladora sector are located in or near the Mexico-U.S. border. New locations somewhat more in the interior of Mexico, yet within easy reach of the U.S. border are developing (e.g., cities such as Chihuahua or Monterrey) as a result of the fierce competition for skilled personnel and services in the northern areas of Mexico.

Industrial parks have also been set up by Mexican private entrepreneurs that offer necessary infrastructure facilities as well as Mexican firms that could be used on a subcontracting basis by foreign companies. The number of industrial parks has doubled in the last five years to 130 parks, each housing at least twenty maquiladora plants. Twenty-nine percent of the total production of this sector is carried out in industrial parks. However, there is no obligation on the part of a foreign investor to locate its in-bond assembly plant in an industrial park. A maquiladora plant can be set up virtually anywhere in Mexico.

REGULATORY AND TAX ENVIRONMENT

One hundred percent foreign ownership is permitted in the maquiladora sector of Mexico. Foreign investors who are not willing to make a sizeable commitment at the outset can benefit from the "Shelter Plan," whereby the whole manufacturing process is subcontracted to another firm (Mexican or foreign) already located in the industrial parks in Mexico. These subcontractors need only to be supplied with the specialist machinery and components, as well as essential management staff by the foreign investor. In this way, foreign investors can assess the costs and productivity of operating in Mexico before embarking on a full-scale in-bond assembly operation there.

Any firm with foreign equity participation that wishes to operate in the maquiladora sector must first obtain authorization from the National Commission on Foreign Investment (CNIE). Automatic CNIE authorization is granted to in-bond enterprises with 100 percent foreign ownership if they are producing only for exports. The sale or transfer to other 100 percent foreign-owned companies in the in-bond sector with at least 75 percent foreign capital requires no authorization. Once CNIE authorization is granted, these firms with foreign capital have to register at the National Foreign Investment Registry (RNIE). Mexican firms may also operate in the maquiladora sector of Mexico as long as they export at least 80 percent abroad. In 1986, 44 percent of the total number of maquiladoras in operation were foreign-owned, 18 percent were joint ventures of Mexican and foreign investors, and 30 percent were wholly Mexican-owned.[2] The Mexican-owned maquiladoras are mainly small-scale enterprises.

All companies that want to operate under maquiladora status must also obtain approval from the Secretariat of Commerce and Industrial Development (SECOFI). To qualify for maquiladora status, the firm must fulfill all the regulatory requirements, tax obligations, as well as the labor restrictions and foreign exchange controls associated with direct foreign investment in Mexico. In addition, it should export at least 80 percent of its output. The maquiladoras are permitted to sell up to 20 percent of their output in the Mexican market, after receiving approval from SECOFI, provided local production of these goods is insufficient and no special program to develop similar industries exists.[3] The appropriate import duty has to be paid on those imported components used for the locally marketed output of the maquiladora. After a firm receives SECOFI approval for its maquiladora status, it must import all authorized items within six months. An extension may be granted under special circumstances, such as the construction of special installations. The firm must commence exporting its product within six months of the date at which it received its imported raw materials. All the raw materials and supplies imported must eventually be assembled/processed.

All maquiladoras must request renewal of the SECOFI registration every two years. At this time, the SECOFI may review whether the firm has complied with its commitments or not.

Tax obligations of foreign-owned maquiladoras are the same as that of any firm with foreign participation operating in Mexico. However, two special incentives are available to those operating in the maquiladora sector:

- Temporary tax-free import of equipment, parts, and raw materials needed to carry out assembly operations. This tax shelter is given for a maximum of two years.
- Payments by in-bond industries for wages, royalties, leasing fees, or rents, and the purchase of Mexican goods and services, other than fixed assets, is carried out using the "controlled" foreign exchange rate.

The corporate profits tax payable by an in-bond assembly firm is small, because it is primarily a cost center and is expected to generate a small profit to enable it to pay staff bonuses. Transferable profits are negligible, because the firm "sells" its output almost at cost to the parent company or a distributor abroad. Hence, the taxable base is almost negligible. This fact makes operating in the maquiladora sector of Mexico particularly attractive for foreign entrepreneurs.

The sharp rise in the number of plants in the maquiladora sector during the last two years would suggest the confidence of foreign investors in the growth potential of this sector. The Government has stepped up its liberalization efforts in the regulatory environment to attract more foreign capital, in general, and has become more promotional towards the maquiladora sector, in particular. However, the fear of increased protectionism in Mexico's major trading partner (the United States) and the need for better infrastructural facilities (transportation, telecommunication and housing), even in the industrial parks, still remain.

NOTES

1. Two specific items in the U.S. Tariff Schedule are relevant in this context: TSUS 806.3 and TSUS 807. Under these laws, only the *value added* by the assembly operations in Mexico are subject to U.S. import duties rather than the full value of the imported goods.

2. Source: Banco de Mexico, "The Mexican Economy," 1988.

3. The stated limit can be negotiated upward. Specific approval criteria for local sales has not been formalized.

Appendix C:
Portfolio Investment in Mexico

In this appendix, the feasibility of portfolio investment by foreigners as a source of financing the balance of payments is examined. There has been a marked increase in the share of portfolio investment by foreigners in Mexico in the 1990s. Investment in the Mexican Stock Market provides another avenue via which foreigners could invest in Mexico in the future as progress is made towards voluntary access to international credit markets. In this appendix, a description of the Mexican Stock Exchange (Bolsa Mexicana de Valores) is provided, along with the regulations imposed on portfolio investment by foreign investors and the types of instruments traded in the market. The potential for conversion funds in attracting funds from abroad is discussed.

THE STOCK MARKET

Founded in 1894, the Bolsa Mexicana de Valores (BMV), located in Mexico City, is the only stock exchange in Mexico. As of 1987, there were 233 companies listed. Table C.1 indicates the behavior of the Mexican Stock Market between 1980 and 1987. Any foreign investor can purchase equities in the Mexican Stock Exchange as long as the regulations and tax obligations associated with foreign investment in Mexico are fulfilled. However, the easiest way for foreigners to buy Mexican equities is through the "Mexico Fund," which is traded on the London and New York stock exchanges.

In 1987, the market capitalization value was $12.7 billion with a trading value of $16.7 billion and turnover ratio of 82.6. Mexico's stock market is extremely thin. Only about twenty-six stocks are highly liquid and can be easily traded, whereas another twenty-three have some liquidity, but rapid purchase and sale of these are not always easy. In 1986, four companies--Frisco, Groupo Pliana, Kimberly Clarke de Mexico, and Vitro-- accounted for 13.4 percent of the total volume traded. As of July 1988, stock trading accounted for only 2.25 percent of the total volume traded in the Mexican Stock Exchange.[1] The rest of the market is accounted for by hedging instruments (such as Petrobonds, Pagafes, silver certificates and the

Table C.1
Mexico - The Stock Market, 1980-87

	1980	1981	1982	1983	1984	1985	1986	1987
Number of Listed Companies	271	240	215	174	178	188	166	233
Market Capitalization								
In Pesos (billion)	302.2	264.9	165.8	432.4	705.0	1547.5	5496.9	27882.4
In Dollars (billion)	13.0	10.1	1.7	3.0	3.7	4.2	6.0	12.7
Trading Value								
In Pesos (billion)	63.1	89.8	37.2	113.3	353.4	1130.9	3700.9	23027.8
In Dollars (billion)	2.8	3.7	0.7	1.1	2.1	4.4	6.0	16.7
Turnover Ratio	20.9	33.9	22.4	30.8	50.1	73.1	67.3	82.6
BMV General Index	14432.2	947.9	677.6	2451.9	4038.4	11197.2	47101.0	105669.9
Percent Change	19.9	-33.8	-28.5	261.8	64.7	177.3	320.6	124.3
IFC EDMB Total Returns Index								
(Dec. 1984 = 100)	323.4	175.0	43.9	88.4	100.0	118.4	236.4	215.7

Source: IFC Emerging Stock Markets Factbook, 1988.

forward market) and instruments like Mexican Treasury Certificates (CETES), Banker's Acceptances, Money Market funds, and promissory notes (Table C.2). Because of the thinness of the stock market, the stock market index (known as the BMV General Index) is a poor indicator of the overall economic performance of the Mexican economy. Government intervention (e.g., the support of some stocks by the Mexican Development Bank--Nafinsa) or speculative moves against some stocks can cause severe volatility in the index.

The volatility of the Mexican Stock Market is clearly illustrated by examining the IFC "Emerging Markets Total Returns Index." This index is calculated by taking a sample of actively traded stocks from the Mexican Stock Market (whose combined market capitalization in the base year represents at least 40 percent of the total stock market capitalization) and calculating the average of the changes in the value of these stocks.[2] The standard deviation changes in this Total Returns Index were very large (50.5 for 1987 and 24.1 for the five-year period 1983-87) showing wide variability in the index from month to month. The standard deviation does not, however, say anything about the magnitude of the changes being large or small, but it does indicate whether the changes are consistently of a similar magnitude or not.[3]

REGULATORY AND TAX TREATMENT OF PORTFOLIO INVESTMENT

Any foreigner can transact in the Mexican Stock Market as long as all acquisitions of stocks in Mexican companies by foreigners are registered within thirty days. On the whole, dividend transfers are permitted as long as general requirements, including taxes and mandatory profit sharing, are met. Dividend payments abroad are subject to a 50 percent withholding tax, although stock dividends representing capitalization of retained earning or surplus are not taxable. Interest income is subject to a 21 percent withholding tax with no deductions.

Tax incentives on portfolio investment are limited. However, portfolio investors abroad do enjoy a tax exemption on long-term capital gains on listed shares.

Table C.2
Instruments Traded in the Mexican Stock Market, Percent of Total Amount Traded

	1985	1986	1987
EQUITY SHARES	4.45	4.89	7.48
FIXED-YIELD INSTRUMENTS			
Short-term:	91.91	91.02	90.66
CETES	77.07	54.30	78.03
Banker's Acceptances	12.90	32.95	8.40
Commercial Paper	1.94	3.59	3.28
Other[1]	0.00	0.18	0.96
Long-term:	3.64	4.09	1.86
Petrobonos	2.69	3.21	1.43
BIBs[2]	0.33	0.16	0.03
Debentures	0.62	0.71	0.40
BOREs[3]	0.03	0.02	–
Other[4]	0	0	0.01
TOTAL (in billion pesos)	25435.6	75676.6	307829.7

1. Includes business paper (Pagare Empresarial and Pagares).
2. Bank indemnity bonds.
3. Urban Renovation bonds.
4. Includes Development Bank bonds and Certificados de Participacion Insobiliaria.

Source: Banco de Mexico, "The Mexican Economy," 1988.

CONVERSION FUNDS AS A VEHICLE FOR PORTFOLIO INVESTMENT

Conversion funds provide another avenue for directing portfolio investment. Two categories of conversion funds are plausible:

- New Money (Cash) Conversion Funds, where investors contribute to a mutual fund and receive shares in the mutual fund, which then converts the foreign currency into Mexican pesos and invests the proceeds in the Mexican Stock Exchange. These are subject to foreign exchange risk.
- Debt Conversion Funds, where investors contribute to a mutual fund and receive shares in the mutual fund, which then purchases LDC debt at a discount from the secondary market. The debt is then converted either directly into equity via a debt-equity conversion, or into local currency first and then investing the proceeds in the Mexican Stock Exchange. Currently, there are no debt conversion funds in Mexico.

Debt Conversion Funds could also take the form of Debt Pooled Venture Capital Funds, where a pool of LDC debt is established by membership share participation are converted into Mexican pesos. These proceeds are then used for investment primarily in venture capital projects, which include start-ups and equity financing for first- or second-stage expansions. Bankers Trust started one such fund (Inverpro) in Mexico on July 1987 in collaboration with the Mexican brokerage house Invermexico, the bank Serfin, and the insurance company Nacional Provincial. However, this fund is only minimally capitalized at present. Currently, foreign participation in these funds cannot exceed 49 percent.

Country funds are typically "closed-ended" in that they issue shares just once for trading in the market. "Open-ended" mutual funds, by contrast, continually issue and redeem shares to meet investor demand.

Apart from the usual risk and return considerations associated with investments in conversion funds, four other characteristics are important:

(a)   capital repatriation restrictions;
(b)   transferability;
(c)   tax treatment;
(d)   alternative access to a country's stock market.

Most funds lock in capital for at least three years. This restriction on capital repatriation is generally more stringent for Debt Conversion Funds than for New Money Conversion Funds. In general, individual investors are more willing than institutional investors to lock in their investments for a few years and to reinvest their dividend income. In Mexico, capital repatriation from investments via debt-equity conversions is not allowed for twelve years.

As for the transferability among offshore investors, in general, the rules associated with New Money Conversion Funds are quite liberal. However, for Debt Conversion Funds, the rules vary on a case-by-case basis. Restrictions may be imposed on the portfolio mix of the conversion funds. In the case of Mexico, any transfer of shares among foreign investors that involves debt capitalization requires authorization from the Government. Investment in the Mexico Fund, which is a New Money (Cash) Fund, does not involve any debt conversion and, therefore, is not subject to the authorization requirement.

Tax treatment of new money funds may also differ from that of Debt Conversion Funds. For example, new investment in Brazil is free of capital gains tax and attracts only a 15% withholding tax on dividends, but both dividends and capital gains on equity purchased through debt conversion are taxed at 25 percent. The demand for equities via country funds will be higher if alternative ways of accessing the stock market for foreign investors are limited.

In May 1988, Mexico's first *stock index fund*[4] (the "Eficas" Fund) was instituted. Eficas is open to foreign investors, and may prove particularly attractive for institutional investors abroad who are presently wary of the closed-end Mexico Fund, and would prefer to avoid the regulatory problems and restrictions involved in direct purchase by foreign investors of Mexican stock. Table C.3 provides a summary of the conversion funds that were recently set up in Mexico (after 1987) in an endeavor to attract foreign portfolio investment. The total capitalization of these funds is still quite small relative to the other capital inflows into Mexico.

The Mexican government, in a effort to encourage new investment, has issued franchises to eighteen venture capital funds under a new investment company act. These are directed to manufacturing, in-bond maquiladoras along the U.S. border, and new industrial parks that can be leased to the maquiladoras.[5]

Table C.3
Recent Conversion Funds in Mexico [1]

Name	Size	Arrangers	Maturity	Investors	Investment targets	Managers
Fondo Inverpro	Less than U.S.$5 million (No fixed limit)	Bankers Trust Mexican houses	Open-ended	Arranging houses	Venture capital	Arranging houses
Formex	Greater than U.S.$250 million	Mexican entrepreneurs	10 years	European and Middle Eastern banks	Real estate and industrial projects	Arrangers
Mexican Recovery Fund	U.S.$25 million	Finamex NMB Bank Merrill Lynch	5 years	Individual investors	Debt-equity Finamex swaps and other projects	

1. These conversion fund were launched in 1987 or later.
Source: Latin Finance (several issues).

THE MEXICO FUND

The Mexico Fund was set up in 1981 (Mexico Fund I) as a diversified, close-end investment company. It is a cash conversion fund whose objective is "long-term capital appreciation through investment in securities, primarily equity, listed on the Mexican Stock Exchange" (as per the prospectus). The original offer price was $12.00 per share. There were two offerings of shares made by the fund, one in 1981 (Mexico Fund I) involving 10 million shares and the other in 1983 (Mexico Fund II). An underwriting discount of $0.79 per share is charged by the fund. As of July 31, 1988, 19.72 million shares of the Mexico Fund were in circulation. The Mexican Fund is listed in the New York and London stock exchanges. As of October 20, 1988, a net asset value (NAV) of $7.40 per share and a closing price of 4-7/8 were quoted in the New York Stock Exchange (NYSE). This makes the discount on the share equal to 34.12 percent. Table C.4 compares the positions of the Mexico Fund in 1987 and 1988.

The securities acquired by the fund may include shares reserved for Mexican nationals. These are held in a Mexican Trust, of which the Mexican development bank, Nacional Financiera, S.A. is the trustee. The CNIE has given authorization to this trust to record its ownership of equity shares as Mexican, even though the Mexico Fund, which is the sole beneficiary of the trust, is a U.S. corporation. The fund will not be able to invest in the National Petroleum company (PEMEX), which is the only entity permitted to engage in most oil- and gas-related activities in Mexico, since it does not issue equity shares. Also, equity investments in electricity and railroads are prohibited. In addition, the CNIE requires at least 60 percent of the Board of Directors of the fund to be citizens and residents of Mexico.

The fund is not permitted to invest more than 5 percent of its total assets in the equity of one issuer or purchase more than 10 percent of the voting equity shares in any firm. It is permitted to invest up to 25 percent of its assets in short-term debt certificates of the Mexican Government. No more than 25 percent of the fund's total assets can be invested in one industry. The fund cannot trade in commodities, commodity contracts, real estate, or real estate mortgages.

Since the fund transacts in peso-denominated securities, its asset portfolio is susceptible to foreign exchange fluctuations. This foreign exchange risk associated with the fund's portfolio is borne by the shareholders of the fund.

Table C.4
Status of the Mexico Fund

	July 1987	1988
Net Asset Value (U.S.$)	13.1	17.33
Discount (%)	26.58	31.79
Shares Traded per month (million)	2.80	1.30
Shares in circulation (million)	19.93	19.72

Source: Nacional Financiera.

No special tax holidays are given to the fund by the Mexican government. Therefore, the tax liability of a shareholder of the Mexico Fund will not be any different from any other foreign investor in Mexico.

Given the restrictions on ownership and control of the Mexico Fund by foreigners, it may very well be easier for interested investors from abroad to pursue other avenues of investment in Mexico rather than through the Mexico Fund (or similar closed-end country funds). These could include the use of debt pooled venture capital funds, Debt Conversion Funds, or simply through direct foreign investment in Mexico.

NOTES

1. Sources: "IFC: Emerging Stock Markets Factbook," 1988; Business International Corp, "IL&T Mexico," June 1987; and Bolsa Mexicana de Valores.

2. The price index is based on changes in prices, adjusted for changes in capitalization that affect price per share, such as a stock split. See "IFC: Emerging Stock Markets Factbook," 1988 for details.

3. The standard deviation of the Total Returns Index will be low whether the index increased by 10 percent each month or by 100 percent every month.

4. The stocks in the fund are based quite closely on the stock weightings in the fifty-two stocks BMV index.

5. Source: "The Reluctant Investors," *Euromoney*, September 1988.

Appendix D:
Data Used for Econometric Analysis

LIST OF VARIABLES USED IN THE REGRESSION ANALYSIS

DFICUUSD   Direct foreign investment in Mexico in millions of current U.S. dollars.

DIFPPGD   First differences of PPGDODUS.

DIFRPUBI   First differences of RPUBGDFI.

DIFRPVTI   First differences of RPVTGDFI.

DIFTDDRS   First differences of TODODDRS.

DODDUM1   Dummy variable, which takes on a value of zero prior to 1982 and one from 1982 onwards. Dummy variable to current represent debt overhang situation.

FXRATEUS   Foreign exchange rate pesos per U.S. dollar (nominal).

GDPMXCUP   GDP at market prices in billions of current pesos.

PPGDODUS   External debt of the Mexican public sector in billions current U.S. dollars.

PUBGDFIP   Public gross fixed capital formation in billions of current pesos.

PVTGDFIP   Private gross fixed capital formation in billions of current pesos.

RPUBGDFI   Ratio of public gross fixed capital formation to Gross Domestic Product (GDP) (%).

RPVTGDFI   Ratio of private gross fixed capital formation to GDP (%).

RTOTGDFI   Ratio of total gross fixed capital formation to GDP (%).

TODODDRS   Total external debt (including short-term and IMF purchases) owed by Mexico in current U.S. dollars.

TOTGDFIP   Total gross fixed capital formation in billions of current pesos.

YEAR   Year-end date.

Table D.1. Mexico: Data Used for the Regression Analysis

YEAR	RPUBGDFI	RPVTGDFI	RTOTGDFI	PPGDODUS	GDPMXCUP	PUBGDFIP	PVTGDFIP	TOTGDFIP	FXRATEUS	DFICUUSD
1950	6.4	6.4	12.8	0.11	44	2.8	2.8	5.6	8.7	53.5
1951	5.5	9.8	15.3	0.12	54	3.0	5.3	8.3	8.7	70.7
1952	5.8	10.4	16.2	0.16	60	3.5	6.2	9.7	8.7	31.2
1953	5.3	8.9	14.2	0.19	62	3.3	5.5	8.8	8.7	38.3
1954	6.0	9.2	15.2	0.23	74	4.4	6.8	11.2	11.3	80.4
1955	5.3	10.1	15.4	0.40	88	4.7	8.9	13.6	12.5	92.9
1956	4.8	12.7	17.5	0.44	99	4.8	12.6	17.4	12.5	97.2
1957	5.1	12.1	17.2	0.51	115	5.9	13.9	19.8	12.5	102.5
1958	5.2	11.2	16.4	0.60	124	6.5	13.9	20.4	12.5	74.2
1959	5.1	10.2	15.3	0.65	134	6.9	14.4	21.3	12.5	65.0
1960	6.0	11.0	17.0	0.81	151	9.0	16.5	25.5	12.5	67.9
1961	6.8	9.0	15.8	0.98	162	11.1	14.6	25.7	12.5	94.1
1962	6.6	8.8	15.4	1.13	176	11.7	15.4	27.1	12.5	90.3
1963	7.6	9.1	16.7	1.32	196	14.8	17.8	32.6	12.5	81.4
1964	7.9	9.5	17.4	1.72	231	18.3	22.0	40.3	12.5	111.7
1965	5.6	11.9	17.5	1.81	252	14.2	30.0	44.2	12.5	153.0
1966	6.2	11.8	18.0	1.89	280	17.4	33.1	50.5	12.5	91.0
1967	7.4	12.0	19.4	2.18	306	22.8	36.8	59.6	12.5	70.0
1968	7.5	11.9	19.4	2.48	339	25.4	40.3	65.7	12.5	108.0
1969	7.6	11.8	19.4	2.94	375	28.5	44.3	72.8	12.5	199.0
1970	7.5	12.2	19.7	4.26	419	31.3	50.9	82.2	12.5	323.0
1971	5.6	12.2	17.8	4.55	452	25.4	55.0	80.4	12.5	307.0
1972	7.7	12.9	20.6	5.06	512	39.2	66.3	105.5	12.5	301.0
1973	8.8	12.9	21.7	7.07	620	54.7	80.2	134.9	12.5	457.0

Table D.1. Mexico: Data Used for the Regression Analysis (continued)

YEAR	RPUBGDFI	RPVTGDFI	RTOTGDFI	PPGDODUS	GDPMXCUP	PUBGDFIP	PVTGDFIP	TOTGDFIP	FXRATEUS	DFICUUSD
1974	8.9	12.2	21.1	9.98	814	72.4	99.5	171.9	12.5	678.0
1975	9.8	12.0	21.8	14.27	988	96.6	118.3	214.9	12.5	610.0
1976	9.0	12.4	21.4	19.43	1,471	132.4	182.0	314.4	15.4	628.0
1977	11.8	7.8	19.6	22.91	1,849	218.2	144.2	362.5	22.6	556.0
1978	11.6	9.5	21.1	26.26	2,337	271.1	222.1	493.2	22.8	829.0
1979	13.2	10.2	23.4	29.76	3,068	404.9	312.9	717.8	22.8	1,332.0
1980	14.1	10.7	24.8	33.81	4,470	630.3	478.3	1,108.6	23.0	2,186.0
1981	14.3	12.1	26.4	52.96	6,128	876.2	741.4	1,617.7	24.5	2,537.0
1982	12.3	10.2	22.5	59.73	9,798	1,205.1	999.4	2,204.5	56.4	1,655.0
1983	11.0	6.6	17.6	66.60	17,879	1,966.7	1,180.0	3,146.7	120.1	461.0
1984	11.3	6.6	17.9	69.40	29,472	3,330.3	1,945.1	5,275.4	167.8	390.0
1985	12.5	6.6	19.1	72.10	47,392	5,924.0	3,127.9	9,051.8	257.0	491.0
1986	12.9	6.5	19.4	76.90	79,536	10,260.1	5,169.8	15,429.9	611.4	1,523.0
1987	13.4	5.5	18.9	81.50	193,612	25,944.0	10,648.7	36,592.7	1,366.7	3,248.0

YEAR	TODODDRS	PPGD8182	TOTD8182	DESDUMMY	DODDUMMY	DIFPPGD	DIFRPUBI	DIFRPVTI	DIFTDDRS
1950	0.1	(56.2)	(82.1)	0	0				
1951	0.1	(56.2)	(82.0)	0	0	0.013	(0.900)	3.400	0.013
1952	0.2	(56.2)	(82.0)	0	0	0.037	0.300	0.600	0.037
1953	0.2	(56.2)	(82.0)	0	0	0.030	(0.500)	(1.500)	0.030
1954	0.2	(56.1)	(81.9)	0	0	0.040	0.700	0.300	0.040
1955	0.4	(55.9)	(81.8)	0	0	0.175	(0.700)	0.900	0.175
1956	0.4	(55.9)	(81.7)	0	0	0.042	(0.500)	2.600	0.042
1957	0.5	(55.8)	(81.6)	0	0	0.070	0.300	(0.600)	0.070
1958	0.6	(55.7)	(81.6)	0	0	0.090	0.100	(0.900)	0.090
1959	0.6	(55.7)	(81.5)	0	0	0.046	(0.100)	(1.000)	0.046
1960	0.8	(55.5)	(81.3)	0	0	0.164	0.900	0.800	0.164
1961	1.0	(55.4)	(81.2)	0	0	0.170	0.800	(2.000)	0.170
1962	1.1	(55.2)	(81.0)	0	0	0.143	(0.200)	(0.200)	0.143
1963	1.3	(55.0)	(80.8)	0	0	0.189	1.000	0.300	0.189
1964	1.7	(54.6)	(80.4)	0	0	0.408	0.300	0.400	0.408
1965	1.8	(54.5)	(80.4)	0	0	0.085	(2.300)	2.400	0.085
1966	1.9	(54.5)	(80.3)	0	0	0.079	0.600	(0.100)	0.079
1967	2.2	(54.2)	(80.0)	0	0	0.289	1.200	0.200	0.289
1968	2.5	(53.9)	(79.7)	0	0	0.306	0.100	(0.100)	0.306
1969	2.9	(53.4)	(79.2)	0	0	0.461	0.100	(0.100)	0.461
1970	6.0	(52.1)	(76.2)	0	0	1.319	(0.100)	0.400	3.023
1971	6.4	(51.8)	(75.7)	0	0	0.283	(1.900)	0.000	0.450
1972	7.0	(51.3)	(75.1)	0	0	0.519	2.100	0.700	0.612
1973	9.0	(49.3)	(73.2)	0	0	2.007	1.100	0.000	1.971

Table D.1. Mexico: Data Used for the Regression Analysis (continued)

YEAR	TODODDRS	PPGD8182	TOTD8182	DESDUMMY	DODDUMMY	DIFPPGD	DIFRPUBI	DIFRPVTI	DIFTDDRS
1974	11.9	(46.4)	(70.2)	0	0	2.904	0.100	(0.700)	2.947
1975	15.6	(42.1)	(66.6)	0	0	4.291	0.900	(0.200)	3.663
1976	20.5	(36.9)	(61.6)	0	0	5.165	(0.800)	0.370	4.910
1977	31.2	(33.4)	(51.0)	0	0	3.481	2.800	(4.570)	10.670
1978	35.7	(30.1)	(46.4)	0	0	3.352	(0.200)	1.700	4.543
1979	42.8	(26.6)	(39.3)	0	0	3.493	1.600	0.700	7.096
1980	57.4	(22.5)	(24.8)	0	0	4.056	0.900	0.500	14.550
1981	78.2	(3.4)	(3.9)	0	0	19.148	0.200	1.400	20.837
1982	86.1	3.4	3.9	0	1	6.769	(2.000)	(1.900)	7.885
1983	93.1	10.2	10.9	0	1	6.870	(1.300)	(3.600)	7.000
1984	94.9	13.1	12.7	0	1	2.800	0.300	0.000	1.800
1985	96.9	15.7	14.7	0	1	2.700	1.200	0.000	1.975
1986	101.1	20.6	18.9	1	1	4.800	0.400	(0.100)	4.225
1987	107.9	25.2	25.7	1	1	4.600	0.500	(1.000)	6.800

Sources: NAFINSA (1977), Statistics on the Mexican Economy, Banco de Mexico, Indicadores Economicos, February 1990 and SHCP, Mexico D.F.

Appendix E:
Details of the Regression and Time Series Analysis of 1950–1987 Mexican Data

Chart E.1
Estimated Autocorrelations for PPG Debt

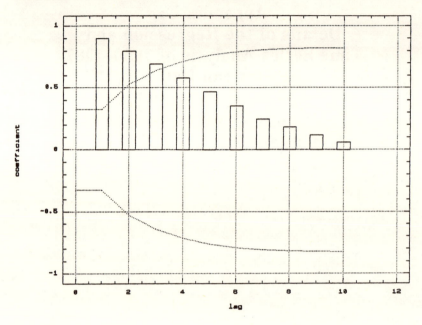

Chart E.2
Estimated Autocorrelations for Total Debt (DRS)

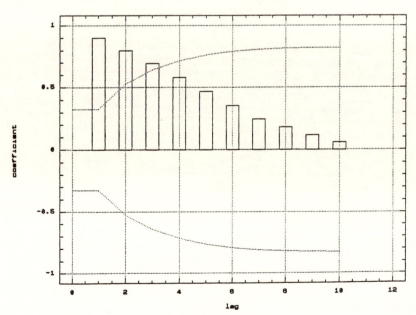

Chart E.3
Estimated Autocorrelations for RPVTGDFI

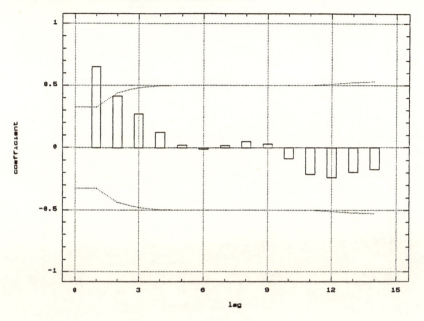

Chart E.4
Estimated Autocorrelations for RPUBGDFI

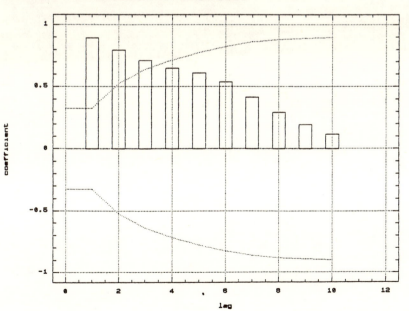

Chart E.5
Estimated Autocorrelations for PPG Debt after First Differencing

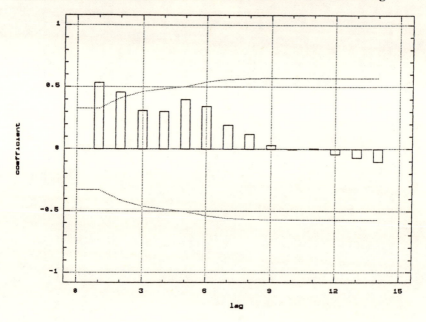

Chart E. 6
Estimated Autocorrelations for Total Debt after First Differencing

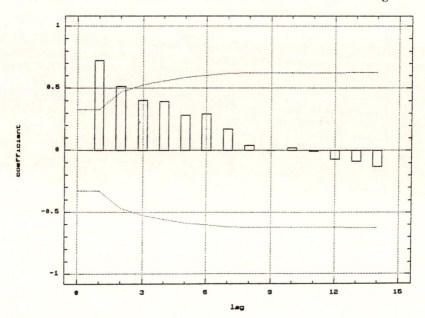

Chart E.7
Estimated Autocorrelations for RPVTGDFI after First Differencing

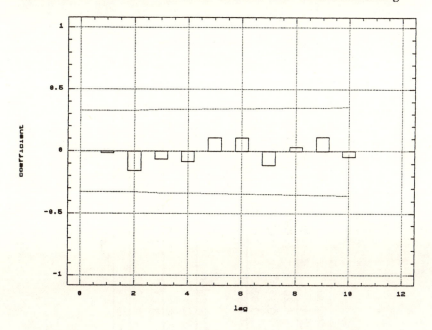

Chart E.8
Estimated Autocorrelations for RPUBGDFI after First Differencing

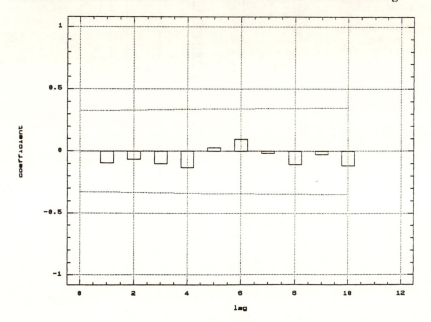

Table E.1 Model Fitting Results for RPVTGDFI

Independent Variable	Coefficient	Standard Error	t-value	Significance level
Constant	9.015	1.203	7.496	0.000
RPUBGDFI	0.301	0.173	1.742	0.090
PPGDOFUS	(0.076)	0.020	(3.866)	0.001
Observations = 38	SE =	1.702	MAE =	1.364

Analysis of Variance for Full Regression

Source	Sum of Squares	DF	Mean Square	F- Ratio	p-value
Model	66.025	2	33.013	11.402	0.000
Error	101.340	35	2.895		
Total (Corr)	167.365	37			

R-Square = 0.394

R-Square (adjusted for d.f.) = 0.360

DW Statistic = 0.900

Table E.2 Model Fitting Results for RPVTGDFI

Independent Variable	Coefficient	Standard Error	t-value	Significance level
Constant	8.872	1.259	7.046	0.000
RPUBGDFI	0.318	0.181	1.751	0.089
TODODDRS	(0.056)	0.015	(3.733)	0.001
Observations = 38	SE = 1.719		MAE = 1.387	

Analysis of Variance for Full Regression

Source	Sum of Squares	DF	Mean Square	F- Ratio	p-value
Model	63.940	2	33.013	11.402	0.000
Error	103.425	35	2.895		
Total (Corr)	167.365	37			
R-Square = 0.382			DW Statistic =	0.859	
R-Square (adjusted for d.f.) = 0.347					

183

Table E.3 Model Fitting Results for DIFRPVTI

Independent Variable	Coefficient	Standard Error	t-value	Significance level
Constant	0.274	0.287	0.954	0.347
DIFRPUBI	(0.371)	0.225	(1.647)	0.109
DIFPPGD	0.003	0.070	0.038	0.970
DODDUM1	(1.442)	0.675	(2.138)	0.040
Observations = 37	SE = 1.418		MAE = 1.030	

Analysis of Variance for Full Regression

Source	Sum of Squares	DF	Mean Square	F- Ratio	p-value
Model	13.742	3	4.581	2.278	0.098
Error	66.368	33	2.011		
Total (Corr)	80.1099	36			

R-Square = 0.172

R-Square (adjusted for d.f.) = 0.096

DW Statistic = 1.879

Table E.4 Model Fitting Results for DIFRPVTI

Independent Variable	Coefficient	Standard Error	t-value	Significance level
Constant	0.336	0.288	1.165	0.253
DIFRPUBI	(0.354)	0.228	(1.553)	0.130
DIFTDDRS	(0.025)	0.053	(0.462)	0.647
DODDUM1	(1.367)	0.653	(2.094)	0.044
Observations = 37	SE = 1.414		MAE = 1.034	

Analysis of Variance for Full Regression

Source	Sum of Squares	DF	Mean Square	F- Ratio	p-value
Model	14.166	3	4.722	2.363	0.089
Error	65.944	33	1.998		
Total (Corr)	80.1099	36			
R-Square = 0.177				DW Statistic =	1.878
R-Square (adjusted for d.f.) = 0.102					

Bibliography

Acharya, Sankarashan and Diwan, Ishac (1989), "Sovereign Debt Buybacks as a Signal of Creditworthiness," World Bank, *PPR Working Papers* No. WPS318, December.

Ahamed, Liaquat (1984), "Oil Exporting Developing Countries Macroeconomic Policies and Adjustment Issues," *World Bank CPD Discussion Paper* No. 1984-87, April.

_____, (1986), "Stabilization Policies in Developing Countries," *The World Bank Research Observer*, Vol. 1, No.1, January, pp. 79-110.

Anand, Ritu and van Wijnbergen, Sweder (1989), "Inflation and the Financing of Government Expenditure: An Introductory Analysis with an Application to Turkey," *The World Bank Economic Review*, Vol 3., No. 1, January, pp. 17-38.

Applegate, Charles and Fennel, Susan (1985) "Cooperating for Growth and Adjustment," *Finance and Development*, December, Vol. 22, No. 4, p. 50.

Arida, Persio (1986), "Macroeconomic Issues for Latin America," *Journal of Development Economics*, Vol. 22, pp. 171-208.

Aspe Armella, Pedro, Rudiger Dornbusch and Maurice Obstfeld (eds.) (1983), "Financial Policies and the World Capital Market: The Problem of Latin American Countries," (NBER Conference Report), Chicago, IL.: University of Chicago Press.

_____, (1986), "Mexico: Growth with Structural Change in the Presence of External Shocks," Mexico D.F.: SPP (mimeo) September.

Balassa, Bela (1981a), *The Newly Industrializing Countries in the World Economy*, New York: Pergamon Press, pp. 83-108.

_____, (1981b), "Policy Responses to External Shocks in Selected Latin American Countries," *Quarterly Review of Economics and Business*, Summer, pp. 131-64.

_____, (1986a), "Policy Responses to Exogenous Shocks in Developing Countries," *American Economic Review*, Papers and Proceedings, May, pp. 75-78.

_____, (1986b), "Economic Prospects and Policies in Mexico," *World Bank*, Development Research Department Discussion Paper #DRD178, May.

Banco de Mexico. "Informe Anual," various issues, Mexico D.F.

_____, "The Mexican Economy," 1985, 1986, and 1988.

_____, "Indicadores Economicos," Mexico D.F. various issues.

Bank for International Settlements (BIS), *Manual on Statistics Compiled by International Organizations on Countries' External Indebtedness*, Monetary and Economics Department.

Banrural (1985), "La Situacion Economica Actual de Mexico 1970-82," Mexico D.F.: Subdireccion General de Programacion y Presupuesto, Mimeo.

Barry, Kenneth (1986), "U.S. Trade Laws Hurting Debtor Nations," *The Mexico City News*, December 5, Mexico D.F.

Barth, James R. and Pelzman, Joseph (1984) "International Debt: Conflict and Resolution," Fairfax, VA.: Dept. of Economics, George Mason University, Working Paper.

Bazant, Jean (1968), "Historia de la Deuda Exterior de Mexico", *Centro de Estudios Historicos*, Mexico: El Colegio de Mexico.

_____, (1981), *Historia de la deuda exterior de Mexico: 1923-1946*, 2nd. ed., Mexico: El Colegio de Mexico.

Berg, Eric (1987a), "Brazil's Action Hurts Bank Stocks," *New York Times*, February 24.

_____, (1987b), "Debt Crisis: Fresh Approaches," *New York Times*, May 6.

Bergsman, Joel (1988) and Edisis, Wayne (1988), "Debt-Equity Swaps and Foreign Direct Investment in Latin America," *IFC Discussion Paper* no. 2, Washington D.C.: International Finance Corporation.

Bergsten, Fred, (1985), William Cline and John Williamson, "Bank Lending to Developing Countries: The Policy Alternatives," *Policy Analyses in International Economics No. 10*, April, Washington, D.C.: Institute for International Economics.

Bird, Graham (1985), "Understanding International Debt," *Journal of Economics*, Summer, pp. 49-56.

Board of Governors of the Federal Reserve System. "The Capital Flight Problem," Discussion Paper #320, Washington, D.C.

Bodayla, Stephen D. (1982), "Bankers vs. Diplomats," *Journal of Inter-American Studies and World Affairs*, Vol. 24, No. 4, November, pp. 461-81.

Borenstein, Eduardo (1990), "Debt Overhang, Debt Reduction and Investment: The Case of Philippines," IMF Working Paper, September, No. WP/90/77.

Brainard, L. J.(1985), "Current Illusions about the International Debt Crisis," *World Economy*, March, 8(1), 1-9.

Branson, William H. (1986), "Stabilization, Stagflation and Investment Incentives: The Case of Kenya, 1979-80," in Edwards, Sebastian and Liaquat Ahamed (eds.), pp. 267-94.

Brau, Williams, Keller and Nowak (1983), *Recent Multilateral Debt Restructurings with Official and Bank Creditors*. Washington,

D.C.: IMF Publication.

Bueno, Gerardo (1971), "The Structure of Protection in Mexico," in Balassa, Bela (ed.), *The Structure of Protection in Developing Countries*, Baltimore: Johns Hopkins University Press.

Buffie, Edward F. (1989) and Allen Sangines Krause, "Mexico 1958-86: From Stabilizing Development to the Debt Crisis," in Sachs, Jeffrey (ed.) National Bureau of Economic Research (NBER) Volume, Washington, D.C., pp. 141-168.

Buira, Ariel (1983), "The Exchange Crisis and the Adjustment Program in Mexico," in John Williamson (ed.) *Prospects for Adjustment*. Washington, D.C.: Institute for International Economics, pp. 51-60.

Buiter, Willem H. (1985), "A Guide to Public Sector Debt and Deficits," and Discussions by Persson, Torsten and Minford, Patrick, in *Economic Policy*, Vol. 1, No. 1, November.

_____, (1988), "Can Public Spending Cuts be Inflationary," NBER Working Paper #2528, Washington, D.C., March.

Bulow, J. and Rogoff, K. (1988), "The Buyback Boondoggle," *Brookings Papers on Economic Activity*, Vol. 2, November, pp. 675-704.

Callier, Philippe (1985), "Further Results on Countries Debt-Servicing Performance: The Relevance of Structural Factors," *Weltwirtschaftliches Archiv*, Band 121, Heft 1, pp. 105-15.

Calvery, John (1985) *Country Risk Analysis*, London: Butterworth and Co., Ltd..

Calvo, Guillermo (1986), *Debt, Stabilization and Development: Essays in Memory of Carlos Diaz Alejandro*, World Institute for Development Economics Research.

Cardoso, Eliana and Levy, Santiago (1988), "Mexico," Ch. 16 in *The Open Economy* by Dornbusch, Rudiger and Helmers, Leslie, F., and Helmers, C. H. (eds.). Washington, D.C.: The World Bank.

Carmichael, Jeffrey (1989), "The Debt Crisis: Where Do We Stand After Seven Years?" *World Bank Research Observer*, July, Vol. 4, No. 2.

Carvounis, Chris C. (1984), *The Debt Dilemma of Developing Nations*, Westport, CT: Quorum Books.

_____, (1986), *The Foreign Debt/National Development Conflict*, Westport, CT: Quorum Books.

Claassen, Emil Maria (1985), "The Lender of Last Resort Function in the Context of National and International Financial Crises," *Weltwirtschaftliches Archiv*, Band 121, Heft 2, pp. 252-60.

Claessens, Stijn and Diwan, Ishac (1990a), "Methodological Issues in Evaluating Debt Reducing Deals." World Bank, *PRE Working Paper*, No. WPS408, May.

_____, and Diwan, Ishac (1990b), "Investment Incentives: New Money, Debt Relief and the Critical Role of Conditionality in the Debt Crisis," *World Bank Economic Review*, Vol. 4, No. 1, January.

_____, Hanna, D. and Lamdany, R. (1990c), "A Note on Appraising Debt and Debt Service Reduction Operations," World Bank, *CFS Informal Financial Note No. 30*, April.

_____, (1990d), "The Debt Laffer Curve: Some Estimates," *World Development*, Vol. 18, No. 12, pp. 1671-1677.

Claudon, Michael P. (ed.) (1986), *World Debt Crisis*, Cambridge, MA.: Ballinger Publishing Co..

Cline, William (1983), "International Debt and the Stability of the World Economy," in *Policy Analyses in International Economics*, No. 4, Institute for International Economics, September.

_____, (1984), *International Debt: Systemic Risk and Policy Response*, Washington D.C.: Institute for International Economics.

_____, (1985), "International Debt: From Crisis to Recovery?" *American Economic Review*, Vol. 75, 2, May, pp. 185-90.

Cohen, B.J. (1985), "International Debt and Linkage Strategies: Some Foreign Policy Implications for the United States," *International Organization* Vol. 39, No. 4, Autumn.

Cohen, Daniel (1985), "How to evaluate the Solvency of an Indebted Nation," *Economic Policy*, No. 1, Vol. 1, November 1985. Discussion by Louka Katseli.

_____, (1990), "Debt Relief: Implications of Secondary Market Discounts and Debt Overhangs," *World Bank Economic Review*, Vol. 4, No. 1, January.

Colaco, F. X. (1985), "International Capital Flows and Economic Development," *Finance and Development*, Vol. 22, No. 3, September, pp. 2-6.

Cooper, Richard N. (1985), *Economic Policy in an Interdependent World: Essays in World Economics*, Cambridge, MA.: MIT Press.

Cordon, Max (1984), "Booming Sector and Dutch Disease Economics: Survey and Consolidation," *Oxford Economic Papers* 36, pp. 359-80.

Dale, Richard S. and Mattione, Richard P. (1983), *Managing Global Debt*. Washington, D.C.: The Brookings Institution.

Datta, Gautam (1984), "Capital Importing Oil Exporters: Structural and Macroeconomic Issues," World Bank CPD Discussion Paper No. 1984-16, June.

Data Resources Inc. (1987), "Latin American Review," First Quarter 1987, Boston, MA: Data Resources.

Davidson, Paul (1987), "A Model Set of Proposals for Resolving the International Debt Crisis," *Journal of Post Keynesian Economics*, Winter 1987-88 Vol. X, No. 2, pp. 323-38.

De Vries, Rimmer (1987), "Commentary on International Debt and Economic Instability" (article by Dornbusch, R.), *Economic Review*, FRB of Kansas City, January, pp. 33.

Debt Crisis Network (1985), *From Debt to Development*, Washington, D.C.: Institute for Policy Studies.

Dervis, Kemal, de Melo, Jamie and Robinson, Sherman (1982), *General Equilibrium Models for Development Policy*. Washington, D.C.: World Bank Research Publication.

Devlin, R. (1984) "The Burden of Debt and the Crisis: Is It Time for a Unilateral Solution," *CEPAL Review*, No. 22, April.

Diaz-Alejandro, Carlos (1981), "Southern Cone Stabilization Plans," in *Economic Stabilization in Developing Countries* by Cline, W. R. and Weintraub, S. (eds.). Washington, D.C.: Brookings Institution.

_____, (1984), "I Don't Think We Are in Kansas Anymore," *Brookings Papers on Economic Activity*, 2, pp. 335-403.

_____, (1987), "Some Aspects of Development Crisis in Latin America," in *Latin American Debt and the Adjustment Crisis* by Thorp, Rosemary and Whitehead, Laurence (eds.), Ch. 2.

Dooley, Michael P. (1987), "Market Valuation of External Debt," *Finance and Development*, March, Vol. 24, No. 1, pp. 6-9.

_____, (1988a), "Analysis of Self-Financed Buybacks and Asset Exchanges," *IMF Working Paper*, WP/88/39, May.

_____, (1988b), "Buybacks and the Market Valuation of External Debt," IMF Staff Papers 35, pp. 215-29.

_____, and Svensson, Lars (1990a), "Policy Inconsistency and External Debt Service," IMF Working Paper No. WP/90/35. April.

_____, (1990b), "A Note on Debt Reduction and Economic Efficiency," *IMF Working Paper*, April, No. WP/90/36.

Dornbusch, Rudiger and Simonsen, Mario Henrique (1983), *Inflation, Debt and Indexation*, Cambridge, MA: MIT Press.

_____, and Fischer, Stanley (1984), "The World Debt Problem," Report to the Group of 24, UNDP/UNCTAD, September.

_____, (1985), "Policy and Performance Links between LDC Debtors and Industrial Nations," *Brookings Papers on Economic Activity*, 2, Washington, D.C.: The Brookings Institution.

_____, (1986), "The Debt Problem and Some Solutions", MIT Working Paper, November.

_____, (1987), "International Debt and Economic Instability", *Economic Review*, Federal Reserve Bank of Kansas City, January, pp. 15.

_____, (1988), "Mexico: Stabilization Debt and Growth," *Economic Policy*, Vol. 7, Issue 1.

Duran, Esperanza (ed.) (1985), *Latin America and the World Recession*, Cambridge: Cambridge University Press, Chs. 1-4, 6, 10.

Eaton, Jonathan and Gersovitz, Mark (1980), "LDC Participation in International Financial Markets: Debt and Reserves," *Journal of Development Economics*, Vol. 7, No. 1, pp. 3-21.

_____, (1981), "Debt with Potential Repudiation: Theoretical and Empirical Analysis," *Review of Economic Studies*, April, 48, 289-309.

Economic Commission for Latin America and the Caribbean (1986a), "The Economic Crisis: Policies for Adjustment, Stabilization and Growth," *Cuadernos de la CEPAL*, October, #LC/G1408/Rev. 2, ECLAC (UN), Santiago, Chile.

_____, (1986b), *Debt, Adjustment and Renegotiation in Latin America*. United Nations.

Edwards, Sebastian (1988), "Terms of Trade, Tariffs and Labor Market Adjustment in Developing Countries," *The World Bank Economic Review*, Vol. 2, No. 2, May, pp. 165-85.

_____, and Ahamed, Liaquat (eds.) (1986), *Economic Adjustment and Exchange Rates in Developing Countries*. NBER Conference Report. Chicago: University of Chicago Press.

_____, and S. van Wijnbergen (1990), "Structural Adjustment and Disequilibrium," in Chenery, H. and Srinivasan T. N. (eds.),

Handbook of Development Economics, New York: North Holland.

Eichengreen, Barry and Lindert, (1989), (ed.), *The International Debt Crisis in Historical Perspective*. Cambridge, MA: MIT Press.

Enders, Thomas and Richard Mattione (1984), *Latin America The Crisis of Debt and Growth*. Washington, D.C.: The Brookings Institution.

Fair, Donald E. and Bertrand, Raymond (eds.) (1983), *International Lending in a Fragile World Economy*. The Hague: Martinus Nijhoff Publishers.

Fischer, Stanley (1986), "Issues in Medium Term Macroeconomic Adjustment," *The World Bank Research Observer*, Vol. 1, No. 2, July, pp. 163-82.

Fishlow, Albert (1985), "Mexico's Integration into the World Economy," in *Mexico and the United States by Musgrave*, Peggy B. (ed.), Boulder, CO: Westview Press, Ch. 8.

Flood, E. (1985), "Currency Risk and Country Risk in International Banking: Discussion," *Journal of Finance*, July, 40(3) pp. 892-93.

Folkeerts-Landau, David and Rodriguez, Carlos A. (1989), "Mexican Debt Exchange: Lessons and Issues," in Frenkel et al. (eds.) *Analytical Issues in Debt*, Washington, D.C.: International Monetary Fund, p. 359.

Froot, Kenneth A. (1989), "Buybacks, Exit Bonds and the Optimality of Debt and Liquidity Relief," *International Economic Review*, Vol. 30, No. 1, February.

_____, and Scharfstein, D., and Stein, J. (1988), "LDC Debt: Forgiveness, Indextation and Investment Incentives," *NBER Working Paper* No. 2541 (March).

Garcia-Alba, Pasqual and Serra-Puche, Jaime (1985), "Economic Fluctuations in Mexico and the United States," in *Mexico and the United States* by Musgrave, Peggy B. (ed.), Boulder, CO: Westview Press, Ch. 4.

Gennotte, Gerard, Kharas Homi and Sadeq, Sayeed (1987), "A Valuation Model for Developing Country Debt with Endogenous Rescheduling," *The World Bank Economic Review*, Vol. 1, No. 2, January.

Gersovitz, Mark (1985), "Banks' International Lending Decisions: What We Know and Implications for Future Research," in Smith, G. and Cuddington, J. (eds.), *International Debt and the Developing Countries*. Washington, D.C.: World Bank, pp. 61-78.

Gil-Diaz, Francisco (1984), "Mexico's Path from Stability to Inflation," in Harberger, A.C. (ed.), *World Economic Growth*, San Francisco, CA: Institute for Contemporary Studies.

_____, (1985a) "Investment and Debt," in *Mexico and the United States* by Musgrave, Peggy B. (ed.), Westview Special Studies in International Economics, Boulder, CO: Westview Press, Ch. 1.

_____, (1985b) "Changing Strategies," in *Mexico and the United States*, by Musgrave, Peggy B. (ed.), Boulder, CO: Westview Press, Ch. 9.

_____, and TERCERO, Raul Ramos (1988), "Lessons from Mexico," in Bruno, M., Di Tella, G., Dornbusch, R. and Fischer, S. (eds.), *Inflation Stabilization*. Cambridge, MA: MIT Press, pp. 361-90.

_____, (1989), "Mexico's Debt Burden," in *Foreign Debt, Adjustment and Recovery* (eds.) Sebastian Edwards, pp. 270-91.

Goldman Sachs Inc. (1987), "LDC Debt Update," *Investment Research*, New York, NY: Goldman Sachs Inc., June.

Gollas, Manuel (1985), "The Mexican Economy at the Crossroads," in External Debt and Development Strategy in Latin America by Antonio Jorge, et al. (eds.), p. 79.

Goode, Richard (1985), *Economic Assistance to Developing Countries through the IMF*. Washington, D.C.: Brookings Institution.

Gooptu, Sudarshan (1989a), "Analysis of Buyback Options in Sub-Saharan Africa," *World Bank CFS Informal Financial Notes Series*, No. 12, Washington D.C., December.

_____, (1989b), "The Market-based Menu Approach in Sub-Saharan Africa: The Tools of Analysis," *World Bank CFS Informal Financial Notes Series*, No. 11, Washington D.C., December.

_____, (1989c), "Direct Foreign Investment in Mexico," *World Bank CFS Informal Financial Notes Series*, No. 6, Washington D.C., March.

_____, (1992) and Richard Brun, "The Role and Cost of Short-term Trade Credit," in *Beyond Syndicated Credits*, Shilling, John (ed.), World Bank Technical Paper No. 163, Washington D.C.: World Bank Publications.

Gordon, David B. and Levine, Ross (1988), "The Capital Flight Problem," Washington, D.C.: Board of Governors Federal Reserve Bank, *International Finance Discussion Paper*, No. 320 (April).

Graham, Bradley (1986), "Country's Improvements Sacrificed for Bank Payments," *The Washington Post*, August 31, 1986.

Granger, C. W. J. (1980), *Forecasting in Business and Economics*. New York: Academic Press Inc.

_____, C. W. J. and Newbold, Paul (1977), *Forecasting Economic Time Series*. New York: Academic Press Inc.

Green, Rosario (1976), *El Endeudamiento publico externo de Mexico 1940-73*. Mexico D.F., Mexico: El Colegio de Mexico.

Gulati, S. (1987), "A note on Trade Misinvoicing," in Donald Lassard and John Williamson (eds.), *Capital Flight and Third World Debt*, Washington D.C.: Institute for International Economics.

Guttentag, Jack M. and Herring, Richard (1985), "The Current Crisis in International Lending," in *Studies in International Economics*, Washington, D.C.: The Brookings Institution.

Hakim, Jonathan (1985), "Latin America's Financial Crisis: Causes and Cures," in *Latin America and the World Recession* in Duran, Esperanza (ed.). Cambridge, U.K.: Cambridge University Press, pp. 17-37.

Harberger, Arnold C. (1986), "Economic Adjustment and the Real Exchange Rate," in *Economic Adjustment and Exchange Rates in Developing Countries* by Edwards, Sebastian and Ahamed, Liaquat (eds.), NBER Conference Report. Chicago: University of Chicago Press.

Hardy, Chandra S. (1982), "Rescheduling Developing Country Debts, 1956-81," *Overseas Development Council* monograph #15, June.

Hay, Johnathan and Bouchet, Michel, (1989), "The Tax Accounting and Regulatory Treatment of Sovereign Debt," (Mimeo), Washington, D.C.: World Bank, for details.

Helpman, Elhanan (1987), "The Simple Analysis of Debt-Equity Swap," mimeo, Cambridge, MA: MIT, September.

International Monetary Fund (1990), "World Economic Outlook," October 1990, Washington D.C.: International Monetary Fund.

Inter-American Development Bank (1985), *Economic and Social Progress in Latin America: External Debt - Crisis and Adjustment*, Washington, D.C., 1985 Report.

Inter-American Development Bank (1984), "*External Debt and Economic Development in Latin America*," Washington, D.C.

Ize, Alain and Ortiz, Guillermo (1987), "Fiscal Rigidities, Public Debt and Capital Flight," *IMF Staff Papers*, Vol. 34, No. 2, June, p. 311.

Katz, Menachem (1989), "Mexico: Anatomy of a Debt Crisis," in Singer, H. W. and Sharma, Sommitra (eds.) *Economic Development and World Debt*. New York: St. Martin's Press.

Kenen, Peter B. (1986), *Financing Adjustment and the International Monetary Fund*. Washington, D.C.: The Brookings Institution, April. Studies in International Economics.

Kharas, H. and Shishido, H. (1986), "A Dynamic Optimization Model of Foreign Borrowing: A Case Study of Thailand," *Journal of Policy Modeling*, 8(1): pp. 1-26.

Kharas, H.J. (1984), "The Long Run Credit-Worthiness of Developing Countries: Theory and Practice," *Quarterly Journal of Economics*, August, pp. 99, 415-40.

Kim, Kwan S. (1985) "Industrial Development in Mexico: Problems, Policy Issues and Perspectives," in Kim, Kwan S. and David, Fk. Ruccio (eds.) *Debt and Development in Latin America*, Indiana: University of Notre Dame Press.

Kindleberger, Charles and Laffargue, J. (eds.) (1982), *Financial Crisis: Theory, History and Policy* Cambridge, MA: Cambridge University Press.

Knox, A. D. (1985), "Resuming Growth in Latin America," *Finance and Development*, Washington D.C.: IMF/World Bank. September, 22(3), pp. 15-18.

Kraft, Joseph (1984), *The Mexican Rescue*, New York: Group of Thirty.

Krayenbuehl, Thomas E. (1985), *Country Risk*, Massachusetts: Lexington Books.

Krueger, Anne O. (1986) "Developing Countries' Debt Problems and Growth Prospects," *Atlantic Economic Journal*, Vol. XIV, No. 1, March.

Krugman, Paul (1985), "International Debt Strategies in an Uncertain World," in Smith and Cuddington (1985), (eds.) *"International Debt and the Developing Countries*. Washington, D.C.: World Bank.

_____, (1988a), "Financing vs. Forgiving a Debt Overhang," *Journal of Development Economics* 2, 9, pp. 253-268.

_____, (1988b), "Market Based Debt-Reduction Schemes," *NBER Working Paper* No. 2587, IMF Staff Papers.

Krugman, Paul (1989), "Market-based Approaches to Debt Reduction," in Dombusch, R., Makin, J. H. and Zlowe, D. (eds.) *Alternative Solutions to Developing Country Debt Problem*. Washington D. C.: American Enterprise Institute for Public Policy Research.

Krugman, Paul and Taylor L. (1978), "Contractionary Effects of Devaluation," *Journal of Development Economics 8*: pp. 445-56.

Lamdany, Ruben (1988), "Voluntary Debt Reduction Operations: Bolivia, Mexico and Beyond," *World Bank Discussion Paper* No. 42, Washington D.C.: World Bank.

_____, (1989), "The Market-Based Menu Approach in Action: The 1988 Brazil Financing Package," *World Bank Discussion Paper* No. 52, Washington D.C.: World Bank.

Lessard, Donald R. and Williamson, John (1985), "Financial Intermediation Beyond the Debt Crisis," in *Policy Analyses in International Economics*, #12 Institute for International Economics, September.

Levin, Ronald and Roberts, David L. (1983), "Latin America's Prospects for Recovery," *Quarterly Review*, FRB of New York, Autumn, Vol. 8, 6-13.

Lombardi, Richard (1985), *Debt Trap* New York: Praeger Publisher.

Looney, R. (1978), *Mexico's Economy.* Boulder, CO: Westview Press.

_____, (1985), *Economic Policymaking in Mexico: Factors Underlying the 1982 Crisis*, Durham: Duke University Press, Ch. 2.

McClellan, Joel (ed.) (1985), *The Global Financial Structure in Transition.* Lexington, MA: Lexington Books.

Maddala, G. S. (1988), *Introduction to Econometrics* New York: Macmillan Publishing Co.

Maddison, Angus (1985), "Two Crisis: Latin America and Asia 1929-38 and 1973-83," OECD Publication, November.

Makin, John H. (1985), *The Global Debt Crisis.* New York: Basic Books, Inc.

Mares, D. R. (1985), "Explaining Choice of Development Strategies: Suggestions from Mexico 1970-1982," *International Organization*,

Vol. 39, No. 4, Autumn, pp.667-97.

Marquez, J. (1985), "Foreign Exchange Constraints and Growth Possibilities in LDC's," *Journal of Development Economics*, Vol. 19, pp. 39-57.

Martinez del Campo, Manuel (1986), *El Desarrollo Industrial De Mexico*, Mexico City : El Colegio de Mexico.

Mendelsohn, M. S. (1983), *Commercial Banks and the Restructuring of Cross-border Debt*. New York, NY: Group of Thirty.

_____, M. S. (1984), *The Debt of Nations* New York: Priority Press Publications.

Mirer, Thad W. (1988), *Economic Statistics and Econometrics*. New York, NY: Macmillan Publishing Co.

Moffett, Matt and Truell Peter (1988), "Mexican Aides Estimate Result of Debt Plan," *Wall Street Journal*, Monday, January 11, 1988.

Morgan Guaranty Trust Co. of New York (1984a), *World Financial Markets*, February 1984.

_____, (1985), *World Financial Markets*, February 1985 --"Argentina."

_____, (1986), *World Financial Markets*, February 1986 -- "The Baker Initiative: The Perspective of the Banks."

_____, (1984b), *World Financial Markets*, October/November 1984--"The LDC Debt Problem -- at the Midpoint."

Mossberg, Walter (1988), "Nations Owed $1.19 Trillion at End of 1987," *Wall Street Journal*, Tuesday, January 19, 1988.

Nacional Financiera, S.A. (1977), "Statistics on the Mexican Economy," Mexico, D.F.

The News, Mexico City Daily Newspaper, various issues.

Nikbakht, Ehsan (1984), *Foreign Loans and Economic Performance* New

York: Praeger.

OECD, 1985 Survey.   "Financing and External Debt of Developing
        Countries, 1985 Survey," OECD, August 1986.   Washington,
        D.C.: OECD Publications.

Oficina de Assesores Del C. Presidente de La Republic.   "XI Reporte
        Grafico Sobre La Economia Mexicana," Mexico D.F. (Historical
        Time Series Data on Mexican Economy).

Ortiz, Guillermo (1991), "Mexico Beyond the Debt Crisis: Towards
        Sustainable Growth with Price Stability," in Bruno, M. Fisher, A.,
        Helpman E. and Liviatan, N. (eds.) *Lessons on Economic
        Stabilization and Its Aftermath*, Cambridge, Mass.: MIT Press.

Ortiz, Guillermo and Serra-Puche Jaime (1986), "A Note on the Burden of
        the Mexican Foreign Debt," *Journal of Development Economics*,
        Vol. 21, 1986, pp. 111-29.

Pearson, David and Lachica, Eduardo (1987), "IMF Creates $8.4 Billion
        Facility For Poorest Nations, Marking Shift," *Wall Street Journal*,
        Wednesday, December 30, 1987.

Pfefferman, G. (1985),   "Overvalued Exchange Rates and Development,"
        Finance and Development 22, March, pp. 17-19.

Philip, George (1985), "Mexico: Learning to Live with the Crisis," in *Latin
        America and the World Recession*, Duran, Esperanza (ed.).
        Cambridge: Cambridge University Press, pp. 81-97.

Pindyck, Robert and Rubinfeld, Daniel (1991), *Econometric Models and
        Economic Forecasts* 3d. ed. New York, NY: McGraw-Hill, Inc.,
        Chs. 15-17.

Ramirez, Miguel (1986), *Development Banking in Mexico.* New York,
        NY: Praeger.

Ranis, Gustav and Orrock, Louis (1985), "Latin American and East Asian
        NIC's: Development Strategies Compared," in *Latin America and
        the World Recession*, Duran, Experanza (ed.).   Cambridge:
        Cambridge University Press, pp. ,48-66.

Reyes, Saul Trejo (1977) "La Politica Laboral," in Gerardo M. Bueno (ed.) *Opcions de Politica Economica en Mexico Despues de la Devaluation*, Mexico D.F.: Editorial Tecnos, p.150

Ros, Jaime (1987), "Mexico from the Oil Boom to the Debt Crisis: An Analysis of Policy Responses to External Shocks, 1978-1985" in *LA Debt and the Adjustment Crisis*, by Thorp, Rosemary and Whitehead, Lawrence (eds.), Pittsburgh, PA: University of Pittsburgh Press.

Sachs, Jeffrey (1983), "Theoretical Issues in International Borrowing,"*NBER Working Paper* No. 1189 Cambridge, MA: National Bureau of Economic Research, August.

_____, (1985), "External Debt and Macroeconomic Performance in Latin America and East Asia," in *Brookings Papers on Economic Activity*, 2, Washington, D.C.: The Brookings Institution.

_____, (1988), "Mexico Plan a Model for Other Debtors," *Wall Street Journal*, Sunday, January 3, 1988.

Sachs, Jeffrey and Cohen, D. (1982), "LDC Borrowing with Default Risk." *NBER Working Paper* 925, New York: National Bureau of Economic Research.

Sangines, Allen (1989), "Managing Mexico's External Debt: The Contribution of Debt Reduction Schemes." World Bank, (mimeo), January.

Scott, Louis (1990), "Pricing Floating-Rate Debt and Related Interest Rate Options." *IMF Working Paper*, No. WP/90/7. February.

Selowsky, M. and Van der Tak, H. G. (1986), "The Debt Problem and Growth," *World Development*, Vol. 14, No. 9, pp. 1107-24.

Shapiro, A. C. (1985) "Currency Risk and Country Risk in International Banking," *Journal of Finance*, July 1985, 40(3), pp. 881-91.

SHCP (1985), "Estrategia de la Restructuracion de la Deuda Externa de Mexico." Bulletin, October 1985, Mexico, D.F.: Secretaria de Hacienda y Credito Publico.

_____, (1986a), "External Debt" (mimeo), Mexico D.F.: Direccion General de Planeacion Hacenderia, CHCP December.

_____, (1986b), "Mexico: Report for Paris Club Discussions," September (mimeo).

_____, (1986c), "Mexico: Development Financing Strategy 1986," September (mimeo).

_____, (1986d), "Informacion de Prensa, No. 241/86" Diciembre 2, de 1986. Mexico D.F.: Press Release of Fiscal Reform Bill presented in Mexican Congress on December 2.

_____, (1986e), "Mexico: Main Economic Issues, SHCP (mimeo).

Simonsen, Mario H. (1985) "The Developing Country Debt Problem," in Smith, G. and Cuddington, J. (eds.), *International Debt and the Developing Countries*, Washington, D.C.: World Bank, pp. 101-26.

Smith, Gordan W. and Cuddington, John T. (eds.) (1985), "International Debt and The Developing Countries," *World Bank Symposium*, Washington, D.C.: World Bank. March.

Solis, Lepoldo and Zedillo, Ernesto (1985), "The Foreign Debt of Mexico," in *International Debt and the Developing Countries*, Smith, Gordon W. & Cuddington, John T. (eds.), Washington, D.C.: World Bank, pp 258-88.

SPFI (1979), "Industrial Development Plan, 1979-1982-1990." Secretaria de Patrimonio y Fomento Industrial (SPFI), Mexico.

SPP (1986), "Nueva Estrategia de Negociacion de la Denda Externa de Mexico," Mexico D.F.: SPP (mimeo) October.

Stewart, Frances (1985), "The International Debt Situation and North-South Relations," in *World Development*, February, p. 191.

Street, J.H. (1985), "Development Planning and the International Debt Crisis in Latin America," *Journal of Economic Issues*, June 19(2) pp. 397-408.

Tanzi, Vito (1986), "Fiscal Policy Responses to Exogenous Shocks in Developing Countries," *American Economic Review*, Papers and Proceedings, May, pp. 88-91.

Tarshis, Lorie (1984), *World Economy in Crisis*. Canadian Institute for Economic Policy.

Taylor, L. (1981), "IS/LM in the Tropics: Diagrammatics of the New Structuralist Macro Critique," in *Economic Stabilization in Developing Countries*, by Cline, W. R. and Weintraub, S. (eds.), Washington, D.C.: Brookings Institution.

Taylor, Lance (1985), "The Crisis and Thereafter: Macro-economic Policy Problems in Mexico," Comments by Reynolds, Clark W. and Schydlowsky, Daniel M. in *Mexico and the U.S.*, by Musgrave, Peggy B. (ed.), Boulder, CO: Westview Press, Ch. 5.

Thorp, Rosemary and Whitehead, Laurence (eds.) (1987), *Latin American Debt and the Adjustment Crisis*. Pittsburgh, PA: University of Pittsburg Press.

Trebat, Thomas J. (1985) "Mexico's Foreign Financing," in *Mexico and the United States* by Musgrave, Petty B. (ed.), *Westview Special Studies in International Economics*, Boulder, CO: Westview Press, Ch. 2.

Trejo-Reyes, Saul (1986), "Deuda-Externa, Una Alternative de Solucion," Mexico D.F.: El Colegio de Mexico, April 1986, Working Paper.

Truell, Peter and Murray, Alan (1987), "Debt Breakthrough," *Wall Street Journal*, Wednesday, December 30, 1987.

United Nations (1975), *"Debt Problems of Developing Countries."* UN Conference on Trade and Development. Report by UN Committee on Invisibles and Financing Related to Trade--Ad hoc Group of Governmental Experts.

Van Wijnbergen, Sweder (1989), "Growth, Debt and the the Real Exchange Rate in Mexico," in Wick A., and Brothers, D. (eds.), *Towards a Development Strategy for Mexico*. Boulder, Co.: Westview Press.

_____, (1990), "Mexico's External Debt Restructuring in 1989-90," *PRE Working Paper* #WP5 424, World Bank, June.

Von Furstenburg, G. M. (1985), "Adjustment with IMF Lending," *Journal of International Money and Finance*, June 4(2), pp. 209-22.

Wallich, Henry (1984), "Insurance of Bank Lending to Developing Countries," Occasional Paper No. 15, New York: Group of Thirty.

Wasserman, U. (1984), "Latin America's Debt Crisis," *Journal of World Trade Law*, July-August, pp. 342-48.

Watkins, Alfred (1986), "Till Debt Do Us Part," Roosevelt Center for American Policy Studies, 1986, Lanham, M.D.: University Press of America.

Weaving, Rachel (1987), "Measuring Developing Countries' External Debt," *Finance and Development*, Washington D.C.: IMF/World Bank. March, Vol. 24, No. 1.

Weintraub, Sidney (1981), "Case Study of Economic Stabilization: Mexico" in *Economic Stabilization in Developing Countries*, Cline, W. R. and Weintraub, S. (eds.), Washington D.C.: The Brookings Institution, Ch. 8, pp. 271-96.

Weisner, Eduardo (1985a), "Latin American Debt: Lessons and Pending Issues," *American Economic Review*, May, Vol.75, No. 2, pp. 191-95.

_____, (1985b), "Domestic and External Causes of Latin American Debt Crisis," *Finance and Development*, March, pp.24.

Williamson, John (1983), "Prospects for Adjustment - In Argentina, Brazil and Mexico," Washington D.C.: Institute for International Economics, June.

_____, (1985), "A Comparision of Macroeconomic Strategies in South America," in *Latin America and the World Recession*, by Duran, Esperanza (ed.), Cambridge: Cambridge University Press, pp.38-47.

Wionczek, Miguel S. (1985), *Politics and Economics of External Debt Crises*, Mexico D. F.: Colegio de Mexico.

Wionczek, Miguel S. (1982), *Some Key Issues for the World Periphery: Selected Essays*, Paragon Press.

World Bank, "World Debt Tables," 1984-85, 1987-88, 1989-90 and supplements. Washington, D.C.: The World Bank.

_____, "World Development Report," 1985, 1986, and 1987, New York: Oxford University Press.

_____, "Annual Report," 1986-89, Washington, D.C.: The World Bank.

Zaidi, Iqbal M. (1985), "Saving, Investment, Fiscal Deficits and External Indebtedness of LDC's," *World Development*, May.

Zedillo, Ernesto (1986a), "The Debt Problem: Notes for Discussion," Mexico, D.F.: Banco de Mexico, mimeo, December.

_____, (1986b), "Capital Flight: Some Observations on the Mexican Case," Presented at the Conference on *Capital Flight and Third World Debt* Washington, D.C.: Institute for International Economics, October 3, 1986.

Index

About the Author

SUDARSHAN GOOPTU is an Economist with the Debt and International Finance Division in the International Economics Department of the World Bank.